the

funny

websites

Zingin.com

An Imprint of Pearson Education

London   New York   Toronto   Sydney   Tokyo
Singapore   Madrid   Mexico City   Munich   Paris

PEARSON EDUCATION LIMITED

Head Office:
Edinburgh Gate
Harlow
Essex CM20 2JE
Tel: +44 (0)1279 623623
Fax: +44 (0)1279 431059

London Office:
128 Long Acre
London WC2E 9AN
Tel: +44 (0)20 7447 2000
Fax: +44 (0)20 7240 5771

First published in Great Britain in 2000

© Paul Carr 2000

ISBN 0-130-32983-5

British Library Cataloguing-in-Publication Data
A catalogue record for this book can be obtained from the British Library.

10 9 8 7 6 5 4 3 2 1

Typeset by Land & Unwin (Data Sciences) Ltd
Printed and bound by Ashford Colour Press, Gosport, Hampshire

The publisher's policy is to use paper manufactured from sustainable forests.

contents

Introduction v

1 The internet: a (very) brief guide 1

2 Relationships and marriage 15

3 Parenting 22

4 Health 28

5 Education 40

6 Employment 62

7 Lifestyle 68

8 Pets and animals 91

9 Useful family advice 96

10 Genealogy 103

Quick reference guide 109

introduction

From education to entertainment, careers advice to counselling, parenting to pets, the internet can help with every
aspect of your family life.

No matter whether you're a busy working mum, a
teenager studying for your GCSEs or a mature student
looking for a university place, the web really does have
something for everyone. The only difficult part is knowing
which sites are worthy of your attention and which are just
a waste of web space.

When we originally launched Zingin.com the plan was
to create a user-friendly, UK-focused, guide to the best of
the web. Although the site itself has grown rapidly since
those early days, we're still very choosy about which sites
we recommend to our users.

With this in mind, when we decided to put this book
together we were determined not to create just another
huge list of family-orientated sites – there's enough of them
around and they just add to the confusion. Instead, we've
tried to provide a user-friendly guide to the best of the
bunch. From educational tools to lifestyle magazines, men's
health to student information – if it's useful and relevant,
you'll find it here; if it's not, you won't.

So who is the book written for? Well, if you're a UK
internet user and want to get straight to the best online
family resources then it's for you! Parents, children,

teenagers, adults – no matter what type of information your family needs, we'll help you to find it.

We've tried to make it as easy as possible for you to just dive in and get started with the book. The chapters have been put in a (hopefully) logical order, starting with finding a partner and getting married, then parenting, health, education and employment, followed by the web's best lifestyle sites, pet care advice, a run-down of some of the most useful sources of family-orientated information and, finally, if you want to look beyond your immediate family, there's even a guide to ways of tracing your ancestors.

Although only the very best of the web has made it into these pages, we've headed up each section with **the best of the best** so you don't have to waste any time getting started – and if you know the name of the site you want, you can look it up in the quick reference section tucked away neatly at the back.

With the help of this book it should be pretty straightforward to find the information you're looking for, but if you do have any problems please come and visit us on the web (**www.zingin.com**) and we'll try our best to help you out.

Enjoy!

Paul Carr
Founder
Zingin.com

the internet:
a (very) brief guide

The fact that you've bought this book means that you've probably used the internet before, either at home or at work. If however you're still getting to grips with the basics then read on for the answers to some of our most frequently asked questions.

Getting started

There are plenty of online resources to help you get the most out of the web, but none of them are any use if you're not online. By far the quickest way to get started is to pop into your local newsagent or computer shop and get hold of one of the zillions of free internet access CDs stuck to the front of popular computer magazines. However, if you want a bit more information before taking the plunge have a quick look at the following pointers.

I'm new to the internet, how do I get started?

It goes without saying that to take advantage of the information contained in this book, you'll need access to the internet. If you want to connect from home you'll need a computer (a 486 or above should be fine), a modem (new computers usually come with one built in) and a spare telephone socket within easy reach of the computer.

The modem, which plugs in to the back of your computer (unless it's already built in) and then into the telephone socket, has basically one purpose – to allow your computer to send and receive data over a telephone line. Once you're plugged in, all that remains now is to decide which internet service provider (ISP) you will use to connect to the net. Your ISP provides a gateway to the internet and, when you ask your computer to connect to the web or to send and receive e-mails, your modem is actually dialling into their network which, in turn, is connected to the rest of the internet. This explains how you can send an e-mail to Egypt or to Edinburgh for the same price – you're only paying for the call to the ISP (the price of a local call or less). If you don't want to connect from home then most large libraries provide free or low-cost internet access, and there are plenty of internet cafés around the country which will be happy to help you take your first online steps.

Which ISP is right for me?

Choosing an ISP can be a complicated business, with some companies offering free access, some with free telephone calls and a few still clinging on to monthly charges – all trying to persuade you that you'll get a better deal with them. Pretty confusing. Basically, the right ISP for you will depend on what you want to use the internet for.

If you're only interested in e-mail, surfing the web and maybe building a personal website, then you'll be fine with a free service. Of course, there's no such thing as a free lunch and you'll usually still have to pay either local call charges or a fixed fee for unlimited access. Luckily for internet users, there's fierce competition between ISPs and you can find some excellent deals if you shop around. To get online with a free service you can either pick up a connection CD from one of the high street shops which have set up their own ISP's (WHSmith, PC World, Waterstone's and Tesco, to name just a few) or call up one of the providers advertised in any of the popular internet magazines.

If you want to use the internet for business and require extra features such as high-speed access, a business website or your own domain name (e.g. **www.yourname.com**) then you'll need use a specialist ISP which will usually charge a monthly fee in addition to your normal phone charges.

If you already have internet access at work, university, school or in a local internet café then visit ISP Review (www.ispreview.co.uk) for a full run-down of the best and worst UK internet service providers.

Online help and advice

OK, so you've made it online and you're looking for help and advice on how to get the most out of the web? Of course, to find the best websites to get you started you'll want to take a quick trip to your friends at Zingin.com (www.zingin.com), but for technical support and general advice, try these.

Why does it say that the page I'm looking for is not found?

The internet is in a constant state of development, and things are getting moved around and deleted all the time. Anyone who's spent more than a couple of minutes on the web will have clicked on a link or typed in a web address only to get hit with the dreaded 'File not found' message. If the page you're looking for seems to have vanished, the most likely cause is that the page has been deleted or moved to another address. If an address doesn't work, try removing bits from the end until you find something. For example, if the address www.asite.com/directory/files/filename.html produces an error, try deleting the 'filename.html' bit to see if there's anything at www.asite.com/directory/files. If you're still getting an error then try www.asite.com/directory and finally www.asite.com. If you run out of things to delete and still can't find the site then it's probably temporarily unavailable or has been deleted. Sites which have been moved can often be tracked down using a search engine such as Google (www.google.com) – simply type in the name of the page/site and see what comes up.

What is the best software for browsing the web?

Most of the free ISPs include a copy of Microsoft internet Explorer on their access CDs and, unless you really want to, there's no real need to use another browser. If you do fancy a change or want to fight back against Microsoft's quest for world domination then there are some alternatives worth trying. The best of the bunch is Netscape Navigator, which contains a very similar range of features as internet Explorer but with slightly less polish. The best way to describe Netscape is like Burger King to Microsoft's McDonald's – try them both and decide which one tastes better. Other choices can be found at **www.browserwatch.com**.

How can I find out more about using the web?

The internet used to be controlled by academics, scientists and computer geeks, and unless you knew your way around it could be very scary indeed. In cyberspace no one could hear you scream.

Nowadays, using e-mail and surfing the web is like driving a car – pretty straightforward when you get the hang of it, even if you don't know exactly what's going on under the bonnet. Having said that, if you want to make the most out of your internet experience you'll need to get a basic grasp of the way it works. One of the best guides to how the net works and what it can do is Learn the Net (**www.learnthenet.com**), which contains some very well-written tutorials covering e-mail, downloading files, building a website and plenty of other useful stuff. If you're baffled by internet jargon you'll definitely want to have a quick look at PC Webopedia (**www.pcwebopedia.com**), and for beginners' advice with a UK perspective visit BBC Webwise (**www.bbc.co.uk/webwise**).

Buying Online

Throughout this book you'll find sites which allow you to order products, book tickets and generally spend your hard-earned cash. The first thing to remember is that using your credit card online is 100% safe providing you take a few sensible precautions.

How do I know which companies to trust?

Firstly, wherever possible stick to companies you've heard of. If someone you know has bought from a particular site without any problems or if it's a household name then the risk is greatly reduced.

As with any purchase on or off the web, you should always ensure that you are buying from a reputable company. Sites such as Amazon (**www.amazon.co.uk**) and Lastminute.com (**www.lastminute.com**) are very well-known internet traders and so are a risk-free option, but if you do want to order from a company you've never heard of then take a look at the next few questions which will hopefully address your concerns.

Can hackers get hold of my credit card number once I've typed it in?

As long as you only type your credit card details into sites which offer encryption security (SSL), your information will be perfectly safe. Look for a yellow padlock on the bottom right of your browser window if you are using internet Explorer or, in Netscape, look for a closed padlock. This ensures that information sent to the site is encrypted and so cannot be intercepted by hackers. If the site is not secure, be very wary about placing an online order and never *ever* send credit card information via normal e-mail.

How can I check on the status of my order?

Many larger sites offer order tracking facilities which allow you to check the progress of your order until it is delivered. If there is no order tracking, ensure there is a contact telephone number in case you need to chase things up.

Is it safe to order from outside the UK?

Orders placed with companies outside the UK are not protected by UK sale of goods or safety legislation. Only order from abroad if you know and trust the company you are dealing with and, even then, try to stick within Western Europe and the USA.

Am I going to get stung by hidden costs?

There's no 'internet tax' for orders made online but, as with any mail order purchase, you should always check whether your order includes postage and packing costs. Also, remember that orders from outside the UK may be subject to additional customs and import costs.

Is there a regulatory body for online traders?

The Consumers' Association has been looking after the interests of shoppers for years and has recently launched a scheme to protect you on the web. The Which? Webtrader scheme (**www.which.net/webtrader**) requires its members to abide to a strict code of conduct if they want to join. Sites which have the Webtrader logo have to provide a decent level of service, otherwise Which? will simply kick them out! It's worth remembering that membership of the scheme isn't compulsory and many reputable businesses are not members, so if you don't see the logo then don't assume the worst, but if you do – expect the best.

What if the goods don't arrive or my credit card is used fraudulently?

Don't panic if products ordered online take a while to arrive. Just like in the real world, delays do happen and things can be out of stock – even if you receive a confirmation saying that everything is fine. However, if you've waited longer than 21 days then you should contact the company concerned to hurry them up.

A gentle reminder will usually be enough to get things moving, but if you're still not getting anywhere you should contact your credit card issuer for advice. If the site is a member of the Which? Webtrader scheme then make sure you let them know as well.

If you have problems with an order made using a credit card, you will usually be able to recover any lost money from your card issuer. If you're concerned about fraud, call your credit card company to check their policy regarding fraudulent transactions.

Can I buy anything I like over the web?

Yes and no. Yes, most things are available – from sweets and cakes to cars and houses but, no, you can't necessarily order them from the UK. The law on ordering from abroad using the internet is the same as using the phone and there are certain products which it is illegal to bring into the country. Some good examples of this are: drugs, certain food items, adult material, pets and automatic weapons. You can probably guess the law's position on drugs and guns but if you need to check out what is allowed, visit Customs and Excise (**www.hmce.gov.uk**).

For the full low-down on internet shopping, check out Zingin's *The very best shopping websites*.

Searching the web

Finding what you're looking for on the internet can be like trying to find a very small needle in a very large haystack. Search engines are fine if you're looking for very specialist information (the population of Peru or the Dutch translation of *Romeo and Juliet*), but when it comes to popular subjects like travel or music it's easy to get swamped by the number of sites available.

So how do you find the information you need without wading through pages of irrelevant junk? Good question.

What is the best search engine?

That all depends on what you're looking for. There are literally thousands of search engines and directory sites and each has its own strengths and weaknesses.

For general searches we recommend Google (**www.google.com**), which ranks sites on both relevance and popularity (how many other sites link to them). You'll usually find the information you want on the first page of results, but if you have no success try the same search on Hotbot (**www.hotbot.com**) and AltaVista (**www.altavista.co.uk**).

If you're looking for UK-specific information there are plenty of home grown search engines which should fit the bill. A couple of our favourites are UK Plus (**www.ukplus.co.uk**) and Search UK (**www.searchuk.co.uk**).

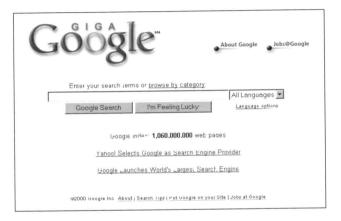

How do I find a business or service?

Looking for a plumber? An electrician? A four-star hotel in Derby? Rather than reaching for the Yellow Pages, take a wander over to Scoot (**www.scoot.co.uk**) which will let you search by business type, location or the name of the company you need. If you prefer to use good old Yellow Pages then it can be found at Yell (**www.yell.com**).

Is it really possible to get free software over the internet? Where can I find it?

The internet is full of free software, much of which can be downloaded for just the price of a telephone call. Generally, unless you are willing to spend some money, you will only be able to get a trial version of the program and it will stop working after a short period of time (usually 30 days). If you want to carry on using it after than you'll have to pay for it – often at a substantial discount over the normal retail price. To get your hands on the best of the freebies, try searching Download.com (**www.download.com**) and Tucows (**www.tucows.com**).

Where can I find the best online shops?

As the number of internet traders has increased, so have the directories who promise to tell you where to find them. One of the most popular shopping directories is Shopsmart (**www.shopsmart.com**), but our personal favourite is 2020 Shops (**www.2020shops.com**) which provides friendly reviews of each of the stores and a useful rating system to help you get started. If you want to compare prices before you buy, you can shop around quickly and easily with the excellent Hoojit (**www.hoojit.com**) or Kelkoo (**uk.kelkoo.com**).

So many search engines, so little time – is there an alternative?

Funny you should ask! You can access the search engines listed above directly from the Zingin Search Guide (**www.zingin.com/guide/search**) and there's a complete listing of UK and global search tools in our Information Guide (**www.zingin.com/guide/info/search**).

Top tips for family safe surfing

How can I stop my children finding unsuitable material on the web?

One of the main concerns about the growth of the internet is the ease with which children can find unsuitable material online. Due to the global and unrestricted nature of the web, it is very easy to find material with an adult theme – some of it illegal under UK law. In order to keep your family safe on the web, there are a number of steps you can take:

- **Install family filter software**

  Companies such as Net Nanny (**www.netnanny.com**) and Cyber Patrol (**www.cyberpatrol.com**) offer software which runs in the background on your computer, restricting access to unsuitable material. However, no software

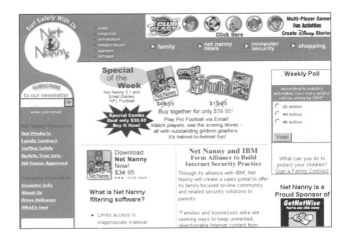

is foolproof and children should always be supervised when surfing the internet.

- **Don't allow unrestricted use of search engines**
  Teaching children to use search engines can improve their computer literacy but also provides quick and easy access to the worst of the web – even the most innocent of searches can return adult results. If children are to be given access to search engines, look for one with a family filter built in which screens out unsuitable results. For UK searches try UK Plus (www.ukplus.com) and for searching the whole web, use the family filter option on AltaVista (www.altavista.com).

- **Chat rooms and e-mail**
  Children often enjoy using the internet to keep in touch with friends through chat rooms or via e-mail. Always take the same precautions with this type of communication as you would with other internet use. The danger of talking to strangers is just as real on the internet as in the real world!

- **Supervise, supervise, supervise**
  As well as being a great way to spend quality time with your family, supervising children while they use the internet is vital to avoid them accessing adult content. For older children, it is often wise to remove the telephone cable from your modem if you are going out and leaving them in the house! As in the real world, however, there are some very real dangers online which can be avoided by simply monitoring your family's internet use.

For more information on keeping your children safe on the internet, check out the excellent Safe Kids (**www.safekids.com**).

"A complete safe-surfing kit and collection of information for parents. This site lays out the rules, the risks, the products and the issues."

– USA Today

SafeKids.Com

Welcome to SafeKids.Com where you'll find tips, advice and suggestions to make your family's online experience fun and productive!

☞Subscribe to our Free e-mail Newsletter

NEW The family that shares a network connection together

Frank Approach to Adolescents and Internet Pornography

relationships and marriage

Before you can start a family, it's pretty important to find someone special to start it with. In this section we concentrate on those early pre-family days – from dating and relating through to actually tying the knot. As with so much else, the internet makes it simple.

Dating

Surfing the web used to be a solitary pursuit. Nowadays, however, people are spending more time in the office and less time socialising and so the internet has become *the* dating tool of choice for millions of people. Of course, the simplest form of e-dating is to ask someone out by e-mail – perfect for the terminally shy, but not so good unless you already know the person you are asking. If, on the other hand, you want to meet someone completely new, you'll want to visit one of the web's increasingly popular dating sites which work in a similar way to traditional dating agencies; you provide some information about yourself, perhaps with a photo, and the service attempts to match you up with someone suitable. Most of the sites do tell you this, but it's worth remembering to be extra careful if you arrange to meet face-to-face someone you've met online – not everyone tells the truth about themselves and, as a rule of thumb, it's not a good idea to give out even your full name or e-mail address unless you know exactly who you're dealing with. See Risks and Hazards of Internet Dating (**www.wildxangel.com**) for some scary but intelligent advice.

■ The best of the best

Secret admirer **www.secretadmirer.com**

Secret Admirer may not be a dating agency in the traditional sense, but it's certainly a godsend for the anyone who can't pluck up the courage to ask someone out. Basically, the site allows you to send an anonymous message to

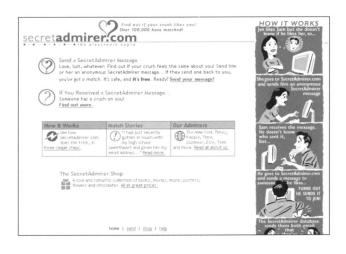

someone you like. The lucky object of your affections receives an e-mail inviting them to send a message to someone *they* like and if, by some amazing coincidence, that person should be you the Secret Admirer database will recognize the match and everyone can live happily ever after. GSOH essential.

■ The rest of the best

Dateline www.dateline.uk.com

As the world's largest, most successful and longest-established introduction agency, you'd expect something pretty special from Dateline. In reality, their site actually looks a little amateurish, with lots of text but a distinct lack of style – it's not obvious whether you're supposed to join before you search the database or search then join. Having said that, appearances aren't everything and the service has a huge number of users with an impressive track record for matching suitable people. If you feel the urge to start right away you can join online, and Dateline's established off-line presence means you needn't have any privacy or security worries. We like.

About Dating dating.about.com

About.com never fails to impress with its personalised guides to every aspect of the internet. As the name suggests, About Dating concentrates on the best online resources for finding someone special – and with hundreds of links, some well-written articles and even discussion forums, it's well worth a visit whether you're desperately seeking a partner or planning that tricky second date. Rather too many American dating stories, but impressive nonetheless.

Personals 365 www.personals365.com

The 365 Corporation continues its quest for online domination with this fresh and funky dating site for the internet generation. Traditionalists will be pleased to hear that the clichéd pictures of happy smiling romantics are still here, but the rest of the service is bang up-to-date with instant registration, real-time chat (no more premium-rate phone calls!) and everything else you need to start meeting new and exciting people. As with most services of this type, there is a monthly charge, but you do get a free trial and it's a price worth paying if you find your soul mate. For an equally modern but thoroughly American alternative, try Match (www.match.com).

Lifestyle.UK Dating www.lifestyle.co.uk/eh.htm

If you've had no luck with our recommended dating agencies, then why not try out some of the other alternatives? This site provides a frighteningly complete list of links to UK dating sites, offering everything from dating for music lovers to Russian brides and even professional alibi services. If you can't find a partner from one of these, then perhaps online dating isn't for you.

■ *The best of the rest*

Dating Direct www.datingdirect.com

Slick, purple and packed to the rafters with dateless hopefuls.

Webpersonals www.webpersonals.com

Tens of thousands of potential partners, all looking for ... erm ... company.

Marriage and weddings

Love and marriage, love and marriage – go together like a horse and carriage. Apparently. OK, things aren't always that straightforward, but if you have managed to find someone to spend the rest of your life with, you'll be pleased to hear that the web can make the happiest day of your life also one of the least stressful. From finding a dress to choosing jokes for the best man's speech – help is only a mouse click away.

■ *The best of the best*

Confetti www.confetti.co.uk

This complete wedding portal offers pretty much everything you could possibly need to organise your big day – advice and ideas, dresses, venues, speeches, stag and hen nights, planning tools, reception planning, gift lists, suppliers and even message boards to swap advice with friends, families and fiancés across the country. Excellent.

■ The rest of the best

Wedding Guide www.weddingguide.co.uk

On first appearances, Wedding Guide looks a bit like the online equivalent of those glossy wedding magazines you see in newsagents – supermodel bride on the cover, screaming headlines offering information and advice, relationship tests to see if it's all a big mistake – you know the drill. Once you get past the front page, however, you'll find a wealth of information for both the bride and groom including advice, services, forums, chat and shopping, all presented in an easy-to-browse format. Where Confetti is definitely a wedding portal, Wedding Guide doesn't seem to be sure whether it's a portal, an e-zine or something else entirely. What is certain, though, is that this award-winning site is well worth a visit.

Wedding Day www.wedding-day.co.uk

More photos of glamorous couples, this time as part of a slick 'n' sexy guide to arranging every aspect of your wedding. From hiring a marquee to choosing the right bridal underwear, all the answers are here – and although there are fewer frills than on some of the other sites, if it's useful and reliable information you're after, you won't find better. For more of the same, with even fewer frills, check out Hitched (www.hitched.co.uk).

Web Wedding www.webwedding.co.uk

A slightly more cluttered approach to the wedding portal business, Web Wedding offers a similar range of features to Confetti but with a more noticeably commercial angle. Shopping aside, the information on offer is first-rate, covering everything from choosing the right music to organising the honeymoon. The shopping's pretty good, too.

Wedding Circle www.weddingcircle.com

Whereas all of the sites reviewed above are UK-based, Wedding Circle is a thoroughly American affair. The great thing about weddings is that, with the exception of a few quirky customs, the advice is the same no matter where you live. With this in mind, the site is well worth a look if you need some tips on arranging photographers, food, speeches, invitations and flowers, although you probably won't be able to take advantage of the impressive services directory, or the online shopping – which isn't really a problem as it's all on Confetti and the rest anyway.

3

parenting

You've found a partner, tied the knot and it's time to start a family. Being a parent is exciting and rewarding but coping with your first child is always going to be a bit stressful, even if you have supportive friends and family to help you out. Fortunately, help is at hand! There are millions of parents around the world who are either going through the same learning process or have done so in the past – and most of them are happy to share tips, tricks and advice with new mums and dads. So the next time you're woken up at four o'clock in the morning or are called into the school to discuss your little angel's behaviour – don't despair, just log on to one of our recommended parenting sites and realise that you're definitely not alone.

Pregnancy and childbirth

If you need some advice before your little bundle of joy arrives on the scene, look no further than these excellent pregnancy sites. For more general health advice, flip straight to Health, Chapter 4.

■ *The best of the best*

The Baby Registry **www.thebabyregistry.co.uk**

No matter whether you're trying for a baby, pregnant or a new parent, The Baby Registry has something for you. From common pregnancy health issues and complaints to getting contraception advice, via chat and shopping, it's all here – and the blokes haven't been forgotten either with their very own 'for dads' section. Nice.

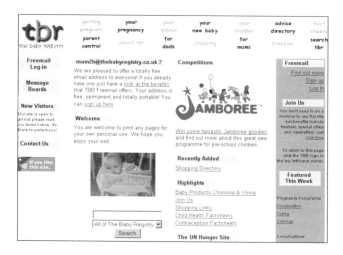

■ *The rest of the best*

Pregnancy Calendar **www.pregnancycalendar.com**

The Pregnancy Calendar is one of those ideas which could only really work properly on the internet. You type in either the conception or due date of your baby and the site builds a day-by-day, fully customised, calendar detailing the development of your little 'un to give you an idea of what to expect and when.

FPA www.fpa.org.uk

Whatever your thoughts on contraception and termination, it's important to have the full facts if you're going to make an informed decision. This excellent site from FPA (formerly the Family Planning Association) presents a very good case for freedom of choice, with plenty of help and advice and details of their latest campaigns. For more of the same, check out the British Pregnancy and Advisory Service (www.bpas.org) while, if you believe that prevention is better than cure, you might want to take a quick look at Condomania (www.condomania.co.uk).

National Childbirth Trust www.nct-online.org

Another charitable site, this time from the National Childbirth Trust which offers support in pregnancy, childbirth and early parenthood. The sheer number of expertly written articles on subjects as diverse as alcohol during pregnancy and coping with colic, combined with photos of newborns with little scrunched-up faces, makes this an essential bookmark for anyone considering, expecting or looking after a baby. By the way, the picture of the smiling male model with the rather confused-looking child wins our 'blatant attempt at gender equality' award. Congratulations to everyone involved.

Child care

Solid food, first steps, starting school – the first few years are as action-packed for your offspring as they are for you. And if you thought that was bad, wait till the teenage years approach – you ain't seen nothing yet! As luck would have it, you can make life easier for everyone concerned by getting a little expert advice, courtesy of the world wide web.

◼ The best of the best

Urbia www.urbia.co.uk

Although Urbia deals with a wide range of family issues, it is particularly strong on providing advice for parents with kids of all ages. From common questions about baby food and nappies to thorny issues like drug abuse and under-age

sex, the site is with you every step of the way. As you might expect, there is a definite women's magazine feel to the whole thing, but the articles are written in such a way that dads shouldn't be put off – the content is excellent and the layout is absolutely faultless. For complete 0–18 coverage, nothing else comes close.

■ The rest of the best

UK Parents www.ukparents.co.uk

Formerly known as UK Mums, this site obviously caved into pressure from the blokes and has now transformed into a cornerstone of gender equality. Name aside, UK Parents is an absolutely invaluable resource for new mums and dads with birth stories, diaries, photos, forums, competitions, advice, recipes and even a parent shop where you can stock up on all those kiddie essentials. From a design point of view, the no-frills layout works very well and navigating is a dream. Like an electronic coffee morning. Without the biscuits. For more of the same, check out Parents Online (www.parents.org.uk).

E-Mum.com www.e-mum.com

Dads? Who are they? This one is purely for the mums, preferably those who are also trying to hold down a job while raising a youngster. The website for the UK's working mums is a slick source of information on a whole range of relevant issues including health, child care, finding a childminder, finding a job and even choosing the right educational books. OK, so most of these features are available on other similar sites, but the bonus here is the continually updated stream of news briefs, keeping you up-to-date with the latest parental news. Function and presentation in equal measure – what more could you ask?

Baby World www.babyworld.co.uk

Over 2500 pages of wonderfully cluttered but beautifully written baby information on all of the usual subjects, plus an extremely well-stocked shop full of all the toys, games and accessories your little one could ever want. The site is part of the Freeserve iCircle network so you'd expect something pretty good – which is exactly what you get here. The advice is first-rate, the production values are equally as good and, if you need any advice, the Baby World experts are on hand to help.

■ *The best of the rest*

Missing Kids www.missingkids.co.uk

Help track down missing children and nail the abductors. Excellent site.

My Family www.myfamily.com

Create a personal homepage for your family. Free and easy to use.

4

health

The web has some excellent health resources in terms of actual medical advice as well as support for those who are suffering from a particular illness or disease, but it's important to tread carefully. Unless you know who's behind a particular site it's probably not a good idea to believe everything you read as anyone can put up a medical website – no recognised qualifications are required. The best advice is to always consult your doctor before acting on any information from the web.

Heath Portals

Health portals have started springing up all over the place in the last couple of years, often fronted by a smiling celebrity doctor and occasionally with the official backing of the NHS or a private healthcare service. No matter how big the doctor's smile or how official the site, it's the quality of information which decides how useful a portal is – and if it's quality information you're after, you'll definitely want to take a quick look at some of these favourites.

■ The best of the best

Net Doctor www.netdoctor.co.uk

Arguably the best health site on the internet, Net Doctor contains more information than you can shake a thermometer at, including an A to Z of diseases, advice on medicines, self tests, health news, discussion and support groups, and even an Ask the Doctor feature where a team of expert doctors, including TV's Dr Hilary Jones, will attempt to answer your medical questions. Whether you want to keep fit and healthy or are about to undergo an operation and want to know what's involved, Net Doctor manages to inform and educate without being too patronising or difficult to understand. Completely indispensable.

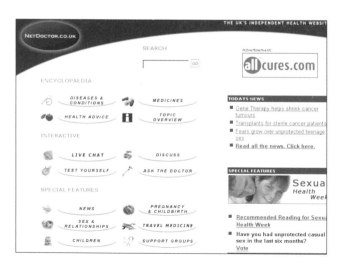

■ *The rest of the best*

BBC Health www.bbc.co.uk/health

The BBC has done it yet again with this excellent health resource. Regardless of your ailment, you'll find information, support, advice and plenty of links to other online medical resources. As with the other BBC sites there are plenty of programme tie-ins, so expect to see the cast of *EastEnders* lecturing you about the importance of exercise and plenty of references to Holby City Hospital.

Health in Focus www.healthinfocus.co.uk

Health in Focus claims to offer 'information, knowledge and choice' to UK patients, health workers and carers, and it broadly achieves this. In addition to the searchable database of health information, there are advice guides, news summaries and plenty of other features to have you back on your feet in no time.

NHS Direct www.nhsdirect.nhs.uk

Excellent health resource designed to cut waiting times. Basically, the site's main role is to determine whether your symptoms are serious enough to warrant a trip to casualty, a ride in an ambulance or whether that stomach pain is just a side-effect of last night's curry. Hypochondriacs will have a field day – while the rest of us will probably want a second opinion.

Surgery Door www.surgerydoor.co.uk

Dr Mark Porter's guide to family heath and fitness is suitably well informed and considerably less smarmy than the good doctor himself.

■ *The best of the rest*

Dr Koop **www.drkoop.net**

Excellent American medical advice site – but would you trust someone called Dr Koop? Didn't think so.

Health Gate UK **www.healthgate.co.uk**

Not exactly the most comprehensive or friendly medical site, but well worth visiting for a second opinion.

Specific advice

From heart disease to first aid, the web is a veritable gold-mine of information about every conceivable complaint, illness, disease and ailment. While you can't beat qualified medical advice from your GP, if you just want some background on a particular condition, allow us to suggest some worthy starting points.

■ *The best of the best*

First Aid **members.tripod.co.uk/rescue**

This site may be an amateur effort but it's difficult to fault the quality of advice on offer. A positive cornucopia of first aid information is provided, from minor cuts and grazes to dealing with phobias and panic attacks. Obviously it's unlikely you'll be able to get to this site when you really need it, so it's well worth spending a couple of hours reading some of the more important sections – just in case. Excellent.

(For the text only version, select this link.)

 FIRST AID
Skill for Life

First aid for the home and office

"First aid Life Saved". Well it may be a little dramatic but sometimes it true.
If you call the emergency medical services to an incident, your actions have started the chain of survival. You have acted to help someone you may not even know. First aid is helping, first aid is making that call, putting a Band-Aid on a small wound, controlling bleeding in large wounds or providing CPR for a collapsed person whose not breathing and heart has stopped. beating. You can help yourself, your loved ones and the stranger whose life may depend on you being in the right place at the right time with the right knowledge. First aid, It's the smart thing to do!

NB.
The information contained on this site should not be used as a substitute for a first aid course or sound medical advice from a Doctor. IEASR and the authors advised all users to consult their own Doctor or Hospital should the need arise. We would also strongly advise people to take a first aid training course with one of the many organisations in their locality.
Information from this site can be downloaded in a file converted to DOC format for 3 com **PalmPilot** hand held computers

Enter Firstaid Site

webfirstaid@iname.com
| Irish Ambulance | Disclaimer:
This site is listed in the BBC Education Web Guide.

■ *The rest of the best*

British Heart Foundation **www.bhf.org.uk**

This excellent resource from the British Heart Foundation provides loads of useful information to help you take care of your heart, including publications, advice and a very useful A to Z of cardiac-related terms. Remember how important it is to look after your heart – you only get one. Unless of course you're Doctor Who.

Meningitis Research Foundation **www.meningitis.org.uk**

An impressive-looking and potentially lifesaving site from the Meningitis Research Foundation offering a wealth of information for anyone concerned about the possibility of contracting the disease. The site is cunningly divided into separate sub-sites for different groups, with information for parents on what to look out for in children and a suitably cool presentation of the same information for 15–25-year-olds. Essential viewing.

The Samaritans www.samaritans.org

Problems and stress can have just as adverse an effect on your health as illness, so it's important to know where to look for help when you need it. The Samaritans have made good use of the web to promote the services they offer as well as providing information about your local branch and useful advice for coping with stress. A impressive site for a lifesaving service. For alcohol worries, check out Alcoholics Anonymous (www.alcoholics-anonymous.org.uk).

Royal National Institute for the Blind www.rnib.org.uk

Contrary to popular belief, the internet can be used by blind and partially sighted people. Special Braille readers and text-to-speech converters make web pages accessible to all and, provided that web designers are considerate with their use of graphics, there's no reason why surfing the web should be any less enjoyable for people without perfect vision. Even if you have no problems with your eyesight, there's enough information here to give you the full story on the institution and its work.

Diabetic Association www.diabetes.org.uk

If you're one of the 1.4 million UK diabetics or just worried that you might be, this official site from the Diabetic Association (formally the British Diabetic Association) provides all of the information you need, including facts about the condition itself, the symptoms, advice for health-care professionals and plenty more.

■ *The best of the rest*

Achoo **www.achoo.com**

Have we missed something? Don't panic, whatever medical information you need, there's almost certainly a link to it here.

Imperial Cancer Research Fund **www.icnet.uk**

Everything from living with cancer to staying safe in the sun. An excellent source of information and advice.

Internet Mental Health **www.mentalhealth.com**

A complete mental health resource designed for professionals but equally fascinating for the rest of us.

Pfizer **www.pfizer.com**

Slick medial advice and information from the people who brought us Viagra. Nice site guys, keep it up.

Healthy eating

Healthy eating isn't just about losing weight, and there are plenty of online resources to help you ensure that you're getting the right balance between the healthy stuff and the less healthy stuff.

■ *The best of the best*

British Nutrition Foundation **www.nutrition.org.uk**

The official nature of the BNF site means you can be pretty sure that the information here is going to be accurate. The features dealing with issues as diverse as 'Chinese Healthy

Eating' and 'Body Image & Eating Disorders', educational information and foundation news are all well-written and informative, but the really useful part is the list of links to relevant informative and educational sites. There's plenty of pictures of fruit, too.

■ *The rest of the best*

The Food Foundation **www.fooddirectory.co.uk**

Another great links directory and plenty of information and advice for consumers. The site is sponsored by Marks & Spencer so it looks a bit special and you can't fault the quality of information – uncluttered and functional.

My Nutrition **www.mynutrition.co.uk**

Plenty of pastel colours (hurray!) on this award-winning 'online guide for everything to do with healthy food, eating

and supplements'. News, a free nutrition consultation and expert advice all ensure that you're enjoying a balanced and nutritional diet. Weight Watchers (**uk.weightwatchers.com**) is probably better for dedicated slimmers, but if you're simply trying to live a healthy life, My Nutrition will certainly set you off on the right track.

Health and beauty shopping

Online health and beauty stores are extremely popular on the other side of the Atlantic and are slowly starting to appear in the UK. High street favourites like Boots (**www.boots.co.uk**) are among the best in the business, but there are plenty of other companies like All Cures (**www.-allcures.com**) who are giving them a serious run for their money so it's well worth shopping around. For a full run-down of Health and Beauty sites, check out *The very best shopping websites*.

■ *The best of the best*

All Cures **www.allcures.com**
All Cures is the UK's first full-service online pharmacy and it's genuinely very impressive. The site is stocked with everything you'd expect to find in your local branch of Boots including over-the-counter medicines, beauty products, toiletries, alternative medicines, photographic services and even NHS and private prescriptions. Obviously if you want them to provide medicine pre-scribed by your GP you'll have to post the prescription to

All Cures (it's a freepost address) to ensure that they get it right – but otherwise everything is available instantly online. The prices compare favourably with high street pharmacies, everything is very well presented and ordering is a doddle – hard to fault really. Love it.

allcures.com

allbeautyproducts.com

Everything men and women need to keep them looking and smelling good.

allpharmacy.com

NHS and Private prescriptions. A full range of Over The Counter Medicines.

allhealth-info.com

Contains health news & features, an A-Z of health and lots more.

alltoiletries.com

Shampoo, deodorant, skincare, dental care - It's all here.

allternative.com

For some natural remedies and vitamin supplements have a look in this part of the store.

allphotoshop.com

For all your photographic needs.

■ *The rest of the best*

Boots www.boots.co.uk

The high street favourite may not have its act together when it comes to selling medicine online, but it's doing pretty well with beauty products and skincare. OK, so it can't compete with All Cures at the moment either on price or range of products, but big companies have a habit of fighting back hard when they feel threatened – and if you already shop at Boots, this is a much simpler way to do it. The site is a combination of shop and magazine, with advice on health, beauty and parenting, plus the opportunity to stock up on everything you need to make you look (and smell) better – you can even collect Advantage Card points if you're into that sort of thing.

Look Fantastic www.lookfantastic.com

While Boots has taken the clutter-free, pastel-coloured design route, Look Fantastic is beautifully busy, with plenty of exclamation marks and unbelievable offers. The big cosmetic names are all here, including Wella, Paul Mitchell and Aveda – some at impressive discounts of up to 60 per cent – and the Which? Web Trader logo will make your shopping less stressful. Bored with simply looking good? Maybe it's time to Look Fantastic.

■ The best of the rest

Avon www.uk.avon.com

The whole Avon range is available on this easy-to-use, if slightly bland, site. There are some pretty reasonable discounts for ordering online.

Iris Online www.iris-online.co.uk

Iris Online provides a simple but very effective way to buy contact lenses without paying over the odds for them. Simply send them your lens prescription and they'll supply everything you need. There's not really much else to say – the site is well laid out, shopping is easy and the prices are great. Sorted.

Condomania www.condomania.co.uk

No more embarrassment in the chemist with this well-designed and well-stocked store. There's a wide range to choose from, and all orders are dispatched in a plain wrapper to avoid knowing looks from the postman. Stop sniggering at the back.

5

education

Learning something new every day just got a whole lot easier thanks to the huge electronic library that is the internet. Pre-school, infant, primary, secondary, higher – it doesn't matter what level you're at, a quick browse through one of our recommended sites will have you on the road to educational enlightenment.

Education portals

Before you start looking into specialist sites for different age groups, it's well worth having a browse through some of the web's largest education portals which offer acres of useful advice and learning aids and will also happily point you towards reference tools, learning resources, schools, colleges, universities and more.

■ The best of the best

BBC Education **www.bbc.co.uk/education**
The BBC has been involved with the web right from the start and, if its current megasite is anything to go by, it'll be at the cutting edge for a long time to come, with education

as one of the cornerstones. From pre-school to higher education, you'll find something for everyone, including plenty of blatant program tie-ins – all in the best possible taste of course – and there's a superb internet guide if you're still a little unsure about all this web malarkey.

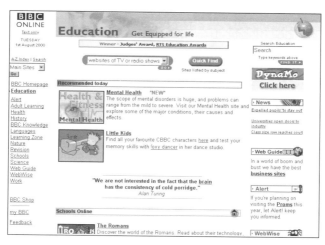

The rest of the best

Learnfree www.learnfree.co.uk

This really is impressive. From pre-school to over-16s, Learnfree is one of the slickest education portals in the business with news, features, advice, forums, polls, revision guides and even cookery tips – if you're a parent you'll wonder how you every lived without it. It's easy to spend hours (weeks?) wandering around the site without even starting to cover everything on offer – but if you're pressed for time, the nursery finder, hot topics and e-mail newsletter are our personal favourites.

Schools Net www.schoolsnet.com

If you're trying to choose the right school, college or university for yourself or your kids then Schools Net could well be the answer to your prayers. Along with an in-depth guide to 22,202 UK schools (count 'em) there's news, book reviews, revision tools, discussion forums and so much more. Very special indeed. For more of the same, with a European flavour, check out European Schoolnet (www.eun.org).

Search Gate www.searchgate.co.uk

This massive directory boasts over 5000 academic, student and careers resources all of which can be searched by category or with the aid of a handy search box. Although there's plenty of subject-related stuff here, the site is particularly strong on information for those in education (students and teachers) – so whether you're looking for advice on your GCSEs or the textbooks you need to complete your degree, this is a great place to start.

Top Marks www.topmarks.co.uk

If Search Gate hasn't provided the site you need, Top Marks is the place to look for a second opinion. Over 1000 high-quality resources are listed along with descriptions, so you know exactly what to expect. It may not be the best education search tool but it looks good and works well. Try it.

Education Unlimited www.educationunlimited.co.uk

The *Guardian*'s network of 'unlimited' sites (News Unlimited, Jobs Unlimited, Cricket Unlimited, etc.) are consistently among the best sites on the web in any particular field, education being no exception. As you'd expect from a newspaper, there is a strong emphasis on educational news as opposed to actually teaching you anything – but if you are a teacher, a student or a parent and you like to know what's going on behind the scenes, this excellent site should be one of your first ports of call.

The Times Educational Supplement www.tes.co.uk

No review of education sites would be complete without mentioning the *TES*. Not only can you read extracts from each week's issue completely free of charge, but this impressive site also offers constantly updated news bulletins and links to other *Times* websites.

The National Grid for Learning www.ngfl.gov.uk

Nothing to do with electricity, the National Grid for Learning is a government initiative designed to allow schools and pupils to share educational resources around the country and even across the globe. The project is still very much in development, but give it a year or so and this could very well be the future of education – and the end of school libraries as we know them.

■ The best of the rest

Advisory Centre For Education www.ace-ed.org.uk

News and information specifically for parents, school governors and teachers.

Parentline Plus www.parentlineplus.org.uk

Ultra-slick charity site offering help and advice to parents and guardians, with online info and a free phone helpline.

No luck?

Still not found the education resource you're looking for? If it's not listed in one of the age-group categories below, make sure you check out Eduweb (**www.eduweb.co.uk**) which is packed full of resources and links to the best of the educational web, surprisingly enough.

Pre-school and infants

Just because they've only just started school doesn't mean that children are too young to start using the internet. Obviously you won't want to let the under-7s wander around unsupervised – but, provided you keep an eye on them, there's no reason why the web shouldn't be an educational goldmine for even the youngest members of the family. For advice on keeping your family safe online, check out the Introduction to this book or visit Net Nanny (**www.netnanny.com**) or Cyber Patrol (**www.cyberpatrol.com**)

■ The best of the best

Fun School **www.funschool.com**

The great thing about pre-school education sites is that the National Curriculum hasn't kicked in yet so, provided there's an educational element and a sense of fun, it's up to the parents to decide what the rules are. With that in mind, this American site is a great resource for both kids and parents, with fun, games and enough child-friendly links to keep the kids clicking until they get to primary school.

■ The rest of the best

Mamamedia www.mamamedia.com

If Fun School doesn't make the grade (sorry) then you'll definitely want to check out Mamamedia. It may be ridiculously bright and garish in design, but it's hard to fault the sheer number of games, toys and general educational activities the site contains. In the unlikely event that you don't find something suitable, you'll be spoilt for choice with over 2000 links to the best of the pre-school web.

Tellytubbies www.bbc.co.uk/education/teletubbies

One of the most controversial children's programs of the past few years. Whether you think that the Tellytubbies are educational marvels or just baby-talking aliens, there's plenty for fans on this colourful official site. Games, biographies and possibly the scariest sun you've ever seen. For more of the same, check out the less student-friendly Tweenies (**www.bbc.co.uk/education/tweenies**).

Winnie the Pooh **www.winniethepooh.co.uk**

A.A. Milne's furry creation has long been an icon for kids around the world – a status which is destined to continue long after technology kills off other low-tech favourites if this excellent site is anything to go by. The first thing to note is that it's an unofficial effort so don't expect any merchandise or references to *The Tigger Movie* – which is possibly a good thing. There are sections on Christopher Robin, A.A. Milne, the characters, games and puzzles, stories and poems and so much more. It may be a fan site, but it puts most official attempts to shame.

Coloring **www.coloring.com**

Every child loves colouring – perhaps some enjoy colouring on the walls and on the sofa more than they enjoy using colouring books but, nevertheless, it's all good fun! Long-suffering parents will be pleased to hear that help is at hand in the form of this excellent no-crayons colourathon. After you've registered on the site (it's free) you simply pick a picture, grab your mouse and start filling in the spaces – and there's no chance of them chewing the crayons.

Big Brainy Babies **www.brainybabies.com**

Got a particularly clued-up bundle of joy? This is the site for you. Brainy Babies contains a whole world of puzzles, trivia and games for young children, although the site's main purpose is to sell you an educational beanbag toy thing. Worth a look.

Primary school

Now we start to get into the realms of the National Curriculum, key stages and all that jazz, so it's a good idea to speak to your child's teacher before you get too heavily into internet learning. Having said that, there are plenty of sites which back up what's taught at school and if you can get them involved in the internet at an early age, children will become more technically literate into the bargain.

■ *The best of the best*

Parents Online **www.parents.org.uk**

Designed to help parents and children through those tricky primary school years, the multi-award-winning Parents

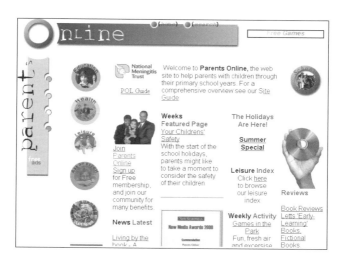

Online contains news, well-written articles, activities, competitions, book reviews, free ads and links to everything else you need to help your children get the best start in education. From mini-beast puppets to meningitis information, this is an excellent place to start.

■ The rest of the best

Bonus www.bonus.com

Bonus is packed full with the usual mix of child-safe surfing and assorted fun stuff – but the neat twist here is their Netscooter, which causes the site to open in a new window, without an address bar or menu options. This means that unless they know their way around internet Explorer it's not easy to wander off to an unsuitable site. If you're using Bonus purely as an educational resource rather than just a way of teaching computer literacy, then bear in mind that as it's based in the USA there may be some information which doesn't fit in with what's taught in UK schools. That aside, the site is great for younger kids and may even keep the adults occupied for a lunch break or two. Oh, and the background music will drive you up the wall. Enjoy.

Ask Jeeves for Kids www.ajkids.com

Web designers seem convinced that children love sites which look like they've been designed by three-year-olds (perhaps they do) – Ask Jeeves for Kids is essentially a search tool which allows children to find stuff on the web using real questions rather than just keywords. No matter whether they're stuck on a tricky homework question or just want to find the official site of their favourite film star,

Jeeves is a great way to teach younger children to search the web without having to worry too much about them finding unsuitable material. Remember, however, the site is American so watch out for tricky spellings for words like 'colour' (color) and 'favourite' (favorite). For more of the same, with a more traditional type of searching, check out Yahooligans! (www.yahooligans.com).

Surf Monkey www.surfmonkey.com

More clunky, chunky design, this time from the bizarrely titled Surf Monkey – a portal which seems to be aimed at a slightly older children than Ask Jeeves for Kids. There are plenty of features, including a guide to cool sites, fun and games, competitions, discussion forums and even the Surf Monkey Club which offers e-mail, chat, bulletin boards and a birthday wish list.

Yucky www.yucky.com

Yucky takes a fun and interactive look at human bodily functions, including burping, farting, spots and nose pick-ing and all those other things which adults disapprove of (in public anyway) and kids can't get enough of. The pro-duction values are top-notch and the information, while it may be a little...erm...in your face, is as accurate as it is engaging. Snot and science? A guaranteed winner.

Homework Solver www.homeworksolver.com

Simply choose a year group, select your subject and you'll be provided with a whole world of advice on answering standard questions. The beauty of the site is that it doesn't answer the question for you – providing instead a gentle shove towards what the teacher is looking for. Great stuff.

Web 66 **web66.coled.umn.edu**

Web 66 lists sites designed by primary schools around the world in a slick, easy-to-browse format, allowing you to easily home in on your local centre of academic excellence to see what they have to offer. If, on the other hand, your local primary isn't listed then there's a whole load of information and advice on how to set up a site for it. Splendid.

Secondary School

By the time your children reach secondary school, they are no longer children – if you see what we mean. OK, so they may not be ready to go out into the big wide world on their own quite yet – but, as far as the web is concerned, there is very little point in trying to strictly control what they do. Family filters will still work up to a point, but most 11-year-olds can get around software protection without too much trouble – supervision is fine but mutual trust is the key. When it comes to SATs, GCSEs and A levels, the internet is far too valuable a resource to be locked away – from English Literature texts to interactive biology textbooks (which are definitely not filter-friendly), the web contains more information than the biggest library or the most expensive set of encyclopaedias. We'll deal with more general reference tools in the cunningly titled General Reference Tools section on p. 57, but, in the meantime, grab your syllabus and prepare to enter a whole new world of learning.

■ The best of the best

BBC Bitesize GCSE www.bbc.co.uk/education/revision

Sometimes you wonder how the BBC does it. It seems that no matter what type of site they build, on whatever subject – from food and drink to football – they do it so unbelievably well that no one else can even come close. Then, of course, you realise that BBC Online has a huge wodge of licence payers' money to play with and suddenly things start to make sense. So what do you get for your licence fee? BBC Bitesize claims to be the 'first ever revision guide via TV, books and the internet', although the well-produced site is probably enough without having to resort to the other media, with nuggets of information and revision tips for pretty much every GCSE subject plus the option to e-mail a teacher if you need help on a particular question. It's free, it works and it looks pretty darn special too. Another winner.

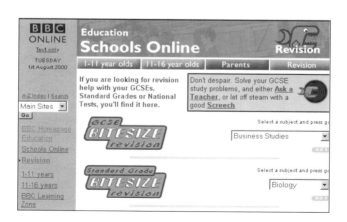

■ *The rest of the best*

Revise It **www.reviseit.com**

GCSEs are the first 'proper' exams most young people will face and so can be enormously hard going, even for the brightest of the bunch. Revise It aims to take some of the stress out of the process by providing revision tips, forums, features and a mutually helpful community of GCSEers who help each other make the most of their revision time. The real prize-winning feature, though, is the revision guide section, which features a wealth of interactive information on all of the key subjects. Students can read summaries of important key topics, highlight important sections on screen and generally use the site as they would use a more traditional textbook – without worrying about out-of-date material and the expense of buying revision books. Revise It is a new site, so some areas are covered better than others – but it's growing every day and certainly deserves to do well.

A Levels **www.a-levels.co.uk**

It may not be as feature-packed as Revise It, but A Levels is still an invaluable resource for anyone studying hard to try and get a decent job or a place at university. At the time of writing, the site was undergoing some pretty major changes so hopefully there will be some exciting new features by the time you visit – but, if not, there are still plenty of categorised links to the best relevant sites and tools on the web. For the same type of thing, but with the focus on GCSEs, check out Project GCSE (**www.projectgcse.co.uk**).

The Learning Shop www.learningshop.com

Despite the slightly naff name (sorry, but it is), this excellent site contains more features than you can shake a well-educated stick at including revision guides, news, study tips and some nifty multimedia stuff. Parents and teachers needn't feel left out either, as the site also boasts a lounge which is almost certainly a hotbed of tea drinking and whinging about your progress (or lack thereof).

Maths Help www.maths-help.co.uk

The concept couldn't be simpler – if you're having trouble with a homework or revision question, you send it to the site and a maths expert will e-mail you with advice on how to go about solving the problem. If you're still stuck then the complete answer is posted on the site a few days later. Almost too good to be true – and where was it when *we* were at school struggling with algebra?

History Channel www.historychannel.com

Although the official site of the History Channel is not specifically aimed at students in secondary education, it provides so much easy-to-digest information that any GCSE or A-level History student will want to bookmark it immediately. Alternatively, for stuff on science and geography, do it like they do on the Discovery Channel (**www.discovery.com**).

New Scientist www.newscientist.com

Like the History Channel and Discovery Channel sites, New Scientist is definitely not just for students but, like the others, it is an invaluable source of background information no matter which exam you're studying for. Up-to-the-minute scientific information, thought-provoking articles and some of the highest standards of presentation and writing on the web make this essential viewing – even if the limit of your scientific aspirations is using a Bunsen burner to set fire to your eyebrows. Love it.

Further and higher education

Going to college or university means much more than simply learning harder stuff – it's about freedom. Freedom to make your own decisions, freedom to learn what you want to learn, freedom to steal traffic cones and drink more than your own body weight in alcohol. The drinking and pilfering aspect is covered later (see Sites for students in Chapter 8) but when you finally get round to the less important matters of choosing a university and actually learning something, make sure you visit some of these handy resources.

■ *The best of the best*

UCAS **www.ucas.ac.uk**

There's no two ways about it – if you're off to college or university, you shouldn't make any decisions until you've checked out this excellent resource from the Universities and Colleges Admissions Service. Our favourite feature is the exhaustive listing of every institution in the UK, complete with information on available courses, contact details and links to their official sites. Also, if you have to get involved with the clearing process, the constantly updated information here will be an absolute godsend. One of that rare breed of official sites which does what it's supposed to do – and much more – with the minimum of fuss and maximum of class.

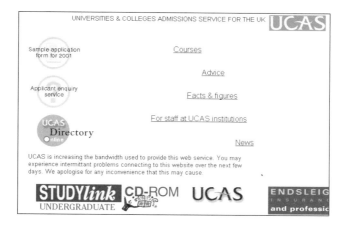

UNIVERSITIES & COLLEGES ADMISSIONS SERVICE FOR THE UK UCAS

Sample application
form for 2001

Courses

Advice

Applicant enquiry
service

Facts & figures

UCAS
Directory
Online

For staff at UCAS institutions

News

UCAS is increasing the bandwidth used to provide this web service. You may
experience intermittant problems connecting to this website over the next few
days. We apologise for any inconvenience that this may cause.

STUDY*link* CD-ROM UCAS ENDSLEIG
UNDERGRADUATE and professic

■ *The rest of the best*

The National Union of Students www.nus.org.uk

Your NUS card is more than just a passport to cheap beer
and cinema tickets, apparently. The National Union of
Students site is full of useful information on student rights
and campaigns, advice on how much money you're entitled
to – and how to get it – plus everything else you need to
fully prepare yourself for higher education. Except perhaps
a love of daytime television and cold pizza – but you'll soon
pick that up.

Hobsons www.hobsons.co.uk

Hobsons has an excellent reputation for providing reliable
information to students, and, like UCAS and the National
Union of Students, its site is an invaluable resource for anyone about to embark on higher education. Essentially the

site is an online guide to courses offered by popular UK universities, but there's also plenty of information on overseas learning and employment as well as some useful leisure guides to help you chill out. A great all-round resource.

Info Youth www.infoyouth.com

Billing itself as a complete guide to opportunities for young people in the UK, Info Youth certainly seems to offer almost everything you could need to get the best start in life. The site is part of the Schools Net network, so when they promise an in-depth guide to every university in Britain you know they *mean* in depth. Not only that but there's also career profiles, gap year opportunities, discussion forums and much more.

Edunet www.edunet.com

Extremely useful search tool, allowing you to find the best courses and institutions around the world. Enter your chosen subject and the country you want to study in and leave the rest to Edunet – simple really.

■ *The best of the rest*

Student Loans Company www.slc.co.uk

Everything you ever wanted to know about the SLC but were too skint too ask.

Unofficial Guides www.unofficial-guides.com

Don't choose a university until you find out what existing students think using this extremely handy resource.

General reference tools

Some of our favourite reference tools which are useful for everyone, regardless of age. On the top of the internet's academic search resources, there are also plenty of reference tools suitable for everyday use including dictionaries and encyclopaedias to answer all of life's questions. For more reference and search tools, check out *The very best searching the internet websites*

◼ *The best of the best*

Britannica **www.britannica.com**

The online version of Britain's favourite encyclopaedia is certainly an impressive affair. Not only will you find the

entire contents of the encyclopaedia, searchable by category and keyword, but there are also expert articles on a range of topical issues, a guide to the best of the web (sounds familiar!), international news stories and even a shop. It's worth noting that the site is actually based in the US so there are more than a few references to American culture and current affairs, but the reference material itself should appeal to everyone. Also, if you feel like spending a few quid in the Britannica shop then you'll need to visit Britannica UK (www.britannica.co.uk) which, at the time of writing, simply consists of a link to the UK shop and another to the American site. All in all a superb reference tool with enough information to satisfy anyone's hunger for knowledge. Great stuff.

■ *The rest of the best*

xrefer www.xrefer.com

'The web's reference engine' is a truly comprehensive affair, allowing you to instantly search a huge number of reference sources, from the *Bloomsbury Dictionary of Contemporary Slang* to the *Oxford Paperback Encyclopedia*, via the *Bloomsbury Guide to Human Thought*. The layout is a simple as you could wish for and the sheer volume of relevant results produced means that you may never need to pick up a dictionary, encyclopaedia or reference book again – oh, and it's British, too!

Encarta www.encarta.com

Encarta started life as a CD-ROM encyclopaedia from the mighty Microsoft but has since evolved into something of a reference monster. Over 16,000 articles are available, representing less than half of the entire database – if you want the rest you'll have to pay – but there's also a dictionary, atlas and plenty of other Microsoft-sponsored content to make up for the shortfall. Like Britannica there's a bit of an American feel here, but if you don't mind replacing *colour* with *color* and *centre* with *center* you'll love it.

The Virtual Reference Desk www.refdesk.com

If you don't fancy the idea of ploughing through loads of reference sites then a quick visit to this simple but effective site, which allows you to search eight popular sources at once, could well be the answer. There's nothing particularly clever about the site and it won't find anything that a direct search wouldn't, but if you want answers and you don't have time to waste it's well worth a look.

Dictionary www.dictionary.com

Simple but very effective, Dictionary will instantly check the spelling and definition of any word you throw at it. To be honest, that's about as far as most people will use the site – but if you do stick around a bit longer, there are plenty of other bits, including tips of usage and style, discussion forums, foreign dictionaries and even a word of the day – just in case you can't think of anything to say. Of course, if you're not happy with the word of the day, you can substitute it for another one on the equally excellent Thesaurus (www.thesaurus.com).

Travlang www.travlang.com

This no-frills site is a great first stop for learning the basics of a foreign language. Once you've chosen where you're travelling to, you are presented with a list of useful phrases which may not make you fluent but will certainly allow you to get by without resorting to mime. For more complex translations, check out Travlang's online dictionaries at **dictionaries.travlang.com**.

Ask A Librarian **www.earl.org.uk/ask**

As if librarians weren't busy enough already, they've now generously given up their time to help internet users track down elusive pieces of information. Using the service is very simple, and very free – you simply type in your question, click the send button and within two working days you'll get an answer. So how does it work? When you ask your question, it is automatically routed to one of the participating UK libraries for a trained librarian to answer. The quality of responses, as you'd expect, is second to none and when you consider that you don't even have to pay for the service, the deal becomes even sweeter – and the best bit is you can talk as loudly as you like while you type your question without the risk of anyone telling you to 'shhhhhhh'.

Multimap **www.multimap.com**

It helps to have a decent map if you're not sure where you're going and Multimap is much more than decent, allowing you to enter any UK postcode or street name and instantly see a detailed map of the area. It's tools like this that make the internet worthwhile.

■ The best of the rest

Encyclopedia.com **www.encyclopedia.com**

Inspired name, inspiring content. Not the best of the bunch, but a great way to find extra back-up information.

Funk and Wagnall's www.funkandwagnalls.com
America's favourite encyclopaedia hits the web.

Google www.google.com
With over one billion web pages listed, Google is quite possibly the world's finest search tool – very useful if you're looking for a very specific piece of information.

6

employment

Just finished school, college or university? Made redundant? Stuck in a rut and looking for a new challenge? We've all heard stories about how good the internet is for helping you find employment – but with a huge number of recruitment and advice sites to choose from, where do you start? Luckily, that's where we come in.

Job hunting

Although there are literally thousands of excellent positions posted online, finding them can be a huge job in itself. As you might expect, technology and media recruitment is extremely popular but even if your dream job is slightly more down to earth, our recommended sites will give you a flying start.

■ The best of the best

Monster **www.monster.co.uk**
Thousands of jobs in a huge range of industries are available from the UK's largest employment site. Monster's US site revolutionised online recruitment on the other side of

the Atlantic, and it was instrumental in doing the same here with a positions database searchable by job title, location, salary and industry. As if offering a huge number of jobs in some of the UK's leading companies wasn't enough there's also plenty of help on offer, including CV tips and tricks, interview advice and everything else you need to get the job you deserve.

■ *The rest of the best*

Gisajob www.gisajob.com

If you don't fancy the idea of trudging around the high street (or the web) visiting hundreds of recruitment companies then you'll love Gisajob, which allows you to search the job listings from over 5000 agencies – all under one roof. The layout may take a bit of getting used to but when you get the hang of how it all works, you'll start to see the beauty of this fast, free and hopefully fruitful resource.

Top Jobs www.topjobs.co.uk

Another major player in the online recruitment world, Top Jobs lists positions in the UK and throughout Europe – allowing you to take advantage of this handy European freedom of movement thing – and also acts as official recruitment agent for some very well-known companies, guaranteeing you an excellent choice of jobs. The front page of the site is absolutely full of information, making it a little difficult to get your bearings, but if you dig deep enough you'll find that the content more than makes up for the design.

Stepstone www.stepstone.co.uk

Still a relative newcomer to the online recruitment arena, Stepstone has zipped up to the top of the tree in record time by offering over 100,000 jobs in the UK and Europe. Like many of the other recruitments services, the service gives you the option of posting your CV online for potential employees to read and, with the number of companies actively using the site growing by the day, you'd be silly not to really.

■ *The best of the rest*

Big Blue Dog www.bigbluedog.com

Nice London-based employment site with a suitably stupid name.

Job Search www.jobsearch.co.uk

Check out over 10,000 vacancies presented in an easy-to-search format.

Jobs Unlimited www.jobsunlimited.co.uk

Position-packed employment site from the *Guardian* offering media, education and social services jobs aplenty.

Reed www.reed.co.uk

Search over 45,000 jobs in a range of industries on this excellent site from one of the high street's most popular recruitment agencies.

Revolver www.revolver.com

Home to thousands of jobs, including those listed in *The Times* and *The Sunday Times*.

Useful resources

Finding a job is the easy part – it's actually getting it that causes the problems. Fortunately the internet can help with that side of things too, with guides to writing the perfect CV, tools enabling you to promote yourself online and even an entire portal dedicated to the art of resignation.

■ *The best of the best*

I-Resign.com www.i-resign.com

Fed up with your job? Now it's easier than ever to resign with the help of the world's first resignation portal. This fantastic-looking site offers advice on quitting, sample resignation letters, discussion boards and even a hall of resignation fame covering a range of celebrity resignations in amusing detail. It's not all fun and frivolity though, as I-Resign.com also provides legal advice to help those who feel hard done by, CV writing advice, financial and taxation information and everything you need to land back on your feet. No matter whether you are seriously considering jacking it in or just want a laugh during your lunch break, this definitely worth a look.

■ The rest of the best

CV Special **www.cvspecial.co.uk**
CV Special isn't a huge site but the information it contains is absolutely invaluable for anyone looking for a new job.

Although the site is basically promoting a business offering CV writing services, it also contains some very handy tips on what makes a good CV (and a bad one), advice on impact and covering letters, and everything you need to know to write your own glowing résumé – so even if you don't want to spend any money, you can give yourself a much better chance of clinching your dream job.

One CV www.one-cv.com

One CV is a great idea, designed to meet the needs of anyone looking for a job on the net. Basically the free service allows you to create an electronic version of your CV which can then be accessed via the web by potential employers using a username and password to guarantee your privacy. Also there's no need for photocopying or stamps – which can only be a good thing.

lifestyle

One of the (many) great things about the internet is that sites can cater for specific groups without having to worry about providing something for everyone. In recent years a number of sites have sprung up which are aimed specifically at men, women, children, teenagers, students, senior citizens and almost every other group of people you can think of. For extremely specialist information, your best bet is to use one of the popular search engines (or pick up a copy of our guide to *The very best ways to search the internet*) – but before you start trawling the web for lifestyle sites, why not check out some of our favourites?

Sites for men

Sites for blokes tend to fall into one of two categories: the lads mag type of site which offers men's health advice, features and a healthy dose of beer, football and women; and the more adult type of site, which doesn't bother with the advice, beer or football. As this is a family book (it even says so on the cover) we'll leave you to find the latter type of site – it isn't difficult – and instead, provide a run-down of the best men's health, advice and lifestyle sites the web has to offer. Be warned, though, most of the following sites do have an adult theme so it's probably best to keep the kids away.

■ *The best of the best*

mens-care.org **www.mens-care.org**

We like this one a lot. Like an electronic men's health handbook, mens-care.org provides in-depth advice on a wide range of issues from prostate problems and cancer to blood pressure problems and healthy eating. Once you've been worried half to death by all of the talk of possible illnesses and diseases, you can even complete an instant assessment to either calm your fears or compound them. Very well put together and a potential lifesaver.

■ *The rest of the best*

FHM **www.fhm.com**

All of the production values and quality articles you'd expect in the paper edition but free of charge and with added interaction. Women, sport, jokes, women, features, film and music reviews, women, editorial, competitions and women. No real surprises but hard to criticise – and apparently they have a pretty substantial female readership too. Something for everyone, then.

Uploaded **www.uploaded.com**

Hot on the heels of FHM, the electronic version of *Loaded* magazine is a little cluttered but more than makes up for it with great depth of content and some thoroughly enjoyable features. A regularly updated front page rant, live webcam, celebrity interviews, competitions and all of the stuff you'd expect to find in the off-line edition make this a great way to spend a lunch break. Needs a good tidy-up though.

Men's Health **www.menshealth.co.uk**

Men's Heath is yet another online version of a popular magazine, but this time the content is a little less focused on the opposite sex. There's a selection of features from the magazine covering health, fitness and sex plus an archive of previous editions, but the main purpose of the site seems to be to sell you a subscription – which is fair enough but not quite as generous as those sites who give most of it away free. For more of the same, check out GQ (**www.swoon.com/ mag_rack/gq.html**).

Boots for Men **www.boots-men.co.uk**

Boots tries to move away from its reputation as a girly beauty shop with this impressive online men's health and beauty store. Hair stuff, face stuff, shaving stuff, bath stuff and more, plus some extremely well-written articles on issues as diverse as smoking and choosing the right hair products. Nice. More of the same is available from The English Shaving Company (**www.theenglishshavingcompany.co.uk**).

■ *The best of the rest*

Boys Stuff **www.boysstuff.co.uk**

'The one stop shop for big boys toys' – not as good as Firebox but well worth a look.

Firebox **www.firebox.com**

Gadgets, gizmos and toys designed especially for blokes. Look out for the La-Z-Boy chair as seen on *Friends* and the ultra-nifty indoor helium airship.

Guy Rules **www.guyrules.com**

Undo millions of years of evolution with this handy guide to being a guy. Sense of humour essential.

Maxim **www.maxim-magazine.co.uk**

You know the drill by now – women, jokes, football and competitions.

Sites for women

Women seem to get a better deal on the web than men. While blokes have a choice of health, sex or both, women get all of that plus lifestyle features, shopping, chat, discussion forums, competitions, support and so much more. Perhaps this is down to the fact that women spend more time chatting online than men, but less time looking at news and sport – or perhaps men are just unlucky. Either way, there are some great women's sites on the web – including these particular favourites.

■ The best of the best

Handbag www.handbag.com

It's not very often that the site which receives the most media coverage is actually the best in its field but, in the case of Handbag, it's very difficult to argue with the hype. Whereas some of the other 'women's portals' prefer to use

flash graphics and pictures of beautiful people rather than any proper substance to attract users, Handbag has got the balance just about right with well-written features on careers, entertainment, fashion, food and drink, health and beauty, home and garden, money, motoring, news, property, relationships, shopping, sport and fitness, technology, travel and more – all presented in a bright and breezy style. Also, before you leave, make sure you drop into the discussion forums to add your thoughts on a range of serious and not so serious issues. Superb.

■ *The rest of the best*

iCircle www.icircle.co.uk

The competition for our best of the best recommendation was extremely fierce and iCircle only narrowly missed out on the top spot. Freeserve's women's channel is packed full of everything you'd expect to find in a traditional women's mag plus loads of interactivity, online shopping, chat, discussions and, of course, access to the whole network of Freeserve sites. As with so many of the other portal sites, everything is arranged into channels including health, relationships, travel, pregnancy and everything else you'd expect – although it's a bit odd that iCircle seems to assume that women wouldn't be interested in things like sport, movies and other non-stereotypical content. Mustn't grumble, though.

Women.com www.women.com

Women.com is based in America and was one of the first sites to concentrate solely on female issues. The range of content is a bit more far-reaching that the UK sites, with channels for entertainment, the internet and politics – although American politics is probably not that high on your list of interests. The layout is superb, the writing is sharp and witty, and if you don't mind talk of presidential elections and diapers, you'll love it.

BEME www.beme.com

The 'first place for women on the web' certainly looks impressive, with beautiful people plastered all over the front page (the cast of *Ally McBeal* when we last looked in) and an ultra-hip (and ultra-slow) navigation system. Speed criticisms aside, the content is impressive enough, with news, entertainment, horoscopes, discussion forums and competitions – and if you have fast internet access at work you'll have hours of fun.

Charlotte Street www.charlottestreet.co.uk

Like BEME, Charlotte Street is another site which tries too hard to be cool at the expense of speed and ease of navigation – but, like BEME, it's also packed with decent content. Well worth a look.

PS Magazine www.psmagazine.co.uk

PS exists both as a normal glossy magazine and also as this equally glossy website. The depth of content may not compare with Handbag and iCircle, but if you're looking for shopping and fashion, it's a thoroughly enjoyable read.

Accessorize www.accessorize.co.uk

If bright nail polishes, novelty hair clips and sarongs are your kind of thing then you'll be in accessory heaven when you visit Accessorize. There's a very '*More* magazine' feel about the site's design, which centres on photos of models who are clearly far too old to be wearing medium stripe flip-flops, and lots of advice on 'how to make the first move on the boy you fancy'.

■ *The best of the rest*

Gal Rules **www.galrules.com**
The girl's version of Guy Rules. Everything you need to know about being a proper girl.

Vogue **www.vogue.co.uk**
Looking for fashion news and plenty of photos? Strike a pose.

Sites for kids

We've already dealt with education in an earlier section, but the web's children's sites are not just about learning – there's plenty of fun to be had, too. From cartoon favourites to fun and games – unlock your inner child and prepare for a world of online fun. For more kids' favourites pick up a copy of *The very best entertainment websites*.

■ *The best of the best*

Children's BBC **www.bbc.co.uk/cbbc**
The BBC has produced some of Britain's best-loved children's programming and some of the UK's best websites, so it seems only natural that when it comes to children's web-

sites they're at the top of the tree. All the favourites are here, including *Newsround* and *Blue Peter* and just about every other CBBC programme – each with its own feature-packed websites complete with news, competitions, games, presented profiles and behind-the-scenes gossip. The production values are second to none, and there's something for all ages – we love it.

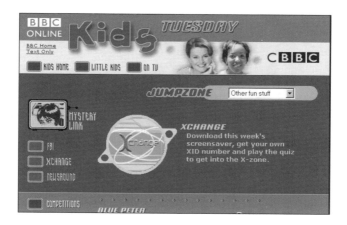

■ *The rest of the best*

CITV www.citv.co.uk

Competing with the BBC for both viewers and site visitors, Children's ITV has put together an impressive site offering programme information, free e-mail, discussion forums and links to the best of the web. It's certainly a bright affair with a bright blue background and plenty of movement but, as a result, navigation could be easier and younger children may have trouble finding their way around. Other than minor gripes, it's difficult to find fault with CITV and kids will love it – which is the main thing, after all.

Kid's Space www.kids-space.org

Younger children will find plenty to see and do on this impressive megasite which offers stories, music, penpals, art galleries, country information and loads of interactive features, all in a child-friendly atmosphere which will keep the youngsters clicking away for hours.

KidsCom www.kidscom.com

For children who have outgrown Kid's Space, KidsCom provides equally engaging content but targeted at a slightly older age group. Penpals and chat, games and fun, polls and forums, links and even the chance to e-mail a world leader about young people's issues. The background music will probably irritate but, other than that, this is an essential bookmark. For more of the same, with a British accent, check out Kids Channel (www.kids-channel.co.uk).

The Simpsons www.thesimpsons.com

Something tells us that the official online home of Homer, Marge and the kids will be equally popular for children and adults. Behind-the-scenes news, character profiles and, unsurprisingly, plenty of animation.

Warner Brothers www.kids.warnerbros.com

More animated action, this time courtesy of Bugs Bunny and friends. Fun, games, movie and cartoon promos and much much more. For even more cartoon fun, check out Disney (disney.go.com).

■ *The best of the rest*

Aardman Animations www.aardman.com

Wallace and Grommit, *Chicken Run* – the gang's all here. For a computer-generated alternative, check out Pixar (www.pixar.com).

Barbie www.barbie.com

Come on Barbie, let's go party. It's all gone very, very pink. To fight back against online girlie oppression, join the fight with Action Man (www.actionman.com).

KidsJokes www.kidsjokes.com

As the name suggests, this bright and colourful site is busting at the seams with jokes. For kids.

Kids Travel www.kidstravel.co.uk

Eliminate holiday boredom with some great ideas for days out. A parental lifesaver.

National Geographic Kids www.nationalgeographic.com/kids

Fun, facts, and activities from the youngster's version of *National Geographic*.

Pokémon World www.pokemon.com

The characters, the cartoons, the comics and, of course, the cards. Gotta catch 'em all.

Sesame Street www.sesamestreet.com

Brought to you today by the letters W, W and W.

Thunk www.thunk.com

Send secret messages to all of your friends with this nifty

site. For some real spying action, check out the CIA Homepage for Kids (**www.odci.gov/cia/ciakids**)

Sites for teenagers

So, you're far too old for kids' sites but still want some web space to call your own? No problem! Look no further than our guide to the best teenage sites on the web.

■ *The best of the best*

The Site **www.thesite.org.uk**
Managing the seemingly impossible task of providing advice and information to young people without patronising or moralising, The Site is an essential visit for anyone concerned about sex, drugs, alcohol, health, money, educa-

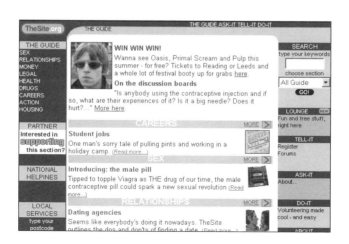

tion and the rest. With contributions from professional counsellors and doctors, you can rest assured that you're getting the best advice and, because it's on the web, the information is free, anonymous and available 24 hours a day. Even if you have no worries (yeah, right!) then The Site is still well worth a look.

■ The rest of the best

Phat Start www.phatstart.com

Phat Start is quite possibly America's finest teenage portal and is another one of the 'by teens for teens' set. Celebrity info, pop culture, sport, homework, gaming, music, fashion, jokes, horoscopes, penpals and even religion are covered in impressive detail, with a network of other Phat sites just a mouse click away. The content on Phat Start is suitable for all but if you want a female-only version, check out Nothing Pink (www.nothingpink.com).

Riot Grrl www.riotgrrl.com

While Riotgrrl is not aimed specifically for teens – and indeed some of it may not be suitable for younger visitors – this attitude-filled girls' site has plenty to offer older teenagers. Smart and sassy features, girl power fashion tips and an unhealthy obsession with Keanu Reeves make this well worth a look for independently minded young women. Zig-ah-zig-ahh.

Teen Today www.teentoday.co.uk

A UK portal and community site put together for teens, by teens. The content is largely sourced from other teen sites but the discussion boards are an excellent way to meet other young people – with a whole range of subjects being discussed every day.

■ *The best of the rest*

Irn Bru www.irn-bru.co.uk

The Irn Bru site is filled with downloads and gimmicks to wind up your friends and waste your workday. From mini-games to spoof e-mails, there's plenty to try out, our particular favourite being the automated robot chat thing that lets you chat to yourself for hours ... and hours ... and hours. Superb.

Monster Teenzone teenzone.monster.co.uk

Get the best start for your career from one of the internet's most impressive employment sites.

Teen Chat www.teenchat.co.uk

Chat to teenagers across the UK. It's always busy and it's completely free.

Sites for students

The best thing about being a student is that you get free high-speed access to the internet. In theory, of course, this is to make research easier but, as any student will testify, it also makes it much easier to check out the best of the web without worrying about internet charges, hefty download times and constant nagging from other people wanting to use the phone. Once you've finished your essay and e-mailed all of your friends – why not chill out in one of our recommended dedicated student portals?

■ *The best of the best*

Student Net **www.student-net.co.uk**

Student Net is one of the largest student portals – and one of the best-looking. Rather than trying to be all things to all people, the site is separated into mini-sites for most of the UK's largest university towns, containing local news and information as well as the more general-interest features. In terms of design, the site is almost faultless with an easy to use navigation system and sharp, quick-loading graphics – and the content isn't bad either, covering entertainment, health, money, chat, competitions and plenty more besides. Not every university town is listed yet but, even if yours is still to come, there's still a great deal to see.

■ *The rest of the best*

Student World www.student-world.co.uk

A close contender for the top spot, Student World is an extremely funky-looking site offering all of the usual features (news, advice and articles) plus a decent amount of 'serious' information about choosing a course, planning your career and generally sorting out your life. If you're looking for an bright and breezy read, you'll want to stick with Student Net – but for a mixture of fun and function, you won't do much better than this.

Student UK www.studentuk.com

The shades-wearing duck tells you straight away that Student UK is concerned with the lighter side of higher education. Yes, there's job information and, yes, there's some excellent advice – but what we like best are the fun bits which include games, competitions, sports news, film and music reviews and shopping. Another great excuse to skip lectures.

Red Mole www.redmole.co.uk

One of the less glossy student sites, Red Mole prefers to concentrate on quality of content rather than flashy design and useless gimmickry. The emphasis here is on creating a community of students with forums, a nonsense exchange (don't ask), polls and even a problem page. It may not be the best-looking site in its field but that won't stop you spending hours and hours using it.

Hot Toast www.hot-toast.co.uk

It's not hot and there's no toast in it, but Hot Toast is still a great place to find student-orientated lifestyle features. The main aim of the service is to provide free internet access, and with their rather nifty online sign-up feature you don't even need a CD – but if you don't fancy changing your internet provider there's loads of other stuff to do on the site, including a decent selection of lifestyle articles, celebrity interviews, competitions and links to other student sites.

■ The best of the rest

Funny www.funny.co.uk

The UK's finest comedy database allows you to search for some of the funniest sites on the web, all sorted into categories to make it easier to have a laugh.

Napster www.napster.com

Exploit your university's bandwidth generosity by downloading free MP3 music. Just don't come running to us if they shout at you.

It's worth mentioning that, at the time of writing, Napster was involved in a tricky copyright-related law suit brought by the big record companies which didn't like the fact that their material was being swapped around. If you get to Napster and find a blank page, you'll know the big record companies won.

Rough Guides travel.roughguides.com

Rough Guides have been kind enough to publish the entire contents of their books on the web, allowing you get a feel for the place you are going to before you leave.

TV Cream www.tv.cream.org

Relive your televisual childhood on this great site. From *Crackerjack* to *Cities of Gold* – it's all here.

The Ultimate Band List **www.ubl.com**

Why waste hours looking for information about your favourite band when The Ultimate Band List will guide you straight to a whole world of official and unofficial shrines to your heroes?

Sites for seniors

Far from being purely a young person's medium, the internet has a huge population of over-50s – so-called 'silver surfers'. To cater for this rapidly expanding group who, let's not forget, control the majority of this country's wealth, there's been a recent explosion in the number of specialist portals offering news, advice, features, forums and shopping for older net users. As with every type of specialist site, the quality of content varies massively, but, if you're looking for a good place to start, you could do a lot worse than some of these.

■ *The best of the best*

Vavo.com **www.vavo.com**

Combing seriously useful features with a certain sense of fun makes Vavo a winner in our book (quite literally). News, education, finance, health and fitness, history, leisure, politics, shopping, travel and work are among the subjects explored on the site, but the real selling point is the huge amount of interactivity on offer. You can use the reunions section to track down long lost friends and family, place an advert in the classifieds section or just set the world to rights in the chat rooms and forums. As refreshing as it is impressive.

Active Lives **www.activelives.co.uk**

If you don't mind the clutter, then you'll find a great deal on offer at Active Lives which doesn't overplay the age card, preferring instead to offer well-written, carefully targeted features which will allow visitors to decide whether the site is aimed at them. The content itself is similar in style to Vavo but with more of a focus on shopping, so it's probably a good idea to keep your credit card away from your computer to avoid temptation. Great stuff.

Saga **www.saga.co.uk**

Synonymous with high-quality over-50s travel, Saga offer holidays to pretty much anywhere on the planet. They've also branched out into insurance, financial services, electrical equipment, nutritional supplements and more, so even if you're not planning on leaving the country, you're bound to find something of interest.

Hairnet www.hairnet.org

The fact that you're reading this book probably means that you have an interest in computers and the web – but if you would like a little extra help with mastering the technology, you'll definitely want to pay a visit to Hairnet. The service offers hands-on computer training to the over-50s and, although it mainly operates in London, there are expert trainers all over the country ready to help you get the most out of you PC – all from the comfort of your own home. Also see the excellent My Hairnet (**www.myhairnet.com**) for a wealth of over-50s information.

Silver Surfers www.silversurfers.net

If you haven't managed to find something suitable on one of the over-50s portals then a quick visit to Silver Surfers is probably in order. Links to the best travel, entertainment, medical, finance, shopping, home, fashion, news (etc.) sites are all just four clicks away from the main front page, so you won't have to spend hours looking for something decent. Cluttered but useful.

■ *The best of the rest*

Women Over 50 www.wo50.com

Useful American site offering information and advice to women who are...er...over 50.

Sites for gays and lesbians

No guide to lifestyle sites could be complete without looking at resources aimed at less traditional family groups.
Surprising as it may seem, not every family consists of hus-
band, wife and 2.4 children – as these recommended sites
ably demonstrate. Please be aware that, as with the male
and female lifestyle resources, some of the following sites
may deal with adult themes and so are probably best left to
the over-18s.

■ The best of the best

About Gay Life gaylife.about.com

Another excellent site from About.com, this time focusing
on a wide range of gay and lesbian issues through well-

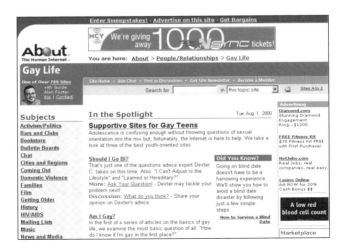

written articles, forums, polls and links to the best of the web. It's based in America and so some of the information may not be totally relevant to UK visitors, but there's more than enough to point you in the right direction.

■ The rest of the best

Gay Life UK www.gaylifeuk.com

A whole host of UK-based gay features including pub and club listings, support pages, news, a chat room, financial information and links to relevant sites and resources. The presentation is little confusing and there are a few adult-themed advertisements dotted around but, all in all, this is a great place to start searching for gay resources. For a more American perspective, check out the ultra-slick Planet Out (www.planetout.com).

Lesbian Nation www.lesbianation.com

As the name suggests, this excellent American site is just for the girls. Extremely high production values are the name of the game here, with extremely well-written content to ensure that it's not a case of form over function. News, features, support, health, forums, postcards, photo galleries, shopping and just about everything you could possibly want make this an essential bookmark.

Gay.com (UK) uk.gay.com

American sites usually have plenty of money to chuck around so you might not be surprised to hear that the fantastic-looking UK Gay.com started life on the other side of the Atlantic. This British version of one of the US's most popular gay resources aims to connect 'the UK lesbian, gay, bisexual and transgender communities' – and, if the quality of articles and range of features on offer are anything to go by, they're doing a pretty good job.

■ *The best of the rest*

Gay Times **www.gaytimes.co.uk**
A whole world of useful resources, designed for a UK audience.

Queer Resources Directory **www.qrd.org**
A no-holds-barred guide to online gay and lesbian content – and with over 25,000 files listed, you're bound to find something of interest.

pets and animals

Just because they have four legs instead of two doesn't make them any the less a part of the family. If you don't have pets you probably won't understand – but, if you do, this one's for you.

Animal advice

No matter whether you have a goldfish or a horse, pets need looking after. Don't worry if you need some help or advice about caring for your pets – it seems that the only thing that animal lovers enjoy as much as caring for their own pets, is helping you to look after yours, as the following sites demonstrate.

■ *The best of the best*

RSPCA www.rspca.org.uk

This bright and friendly site from the RSCPA contains a wealth of information about animals of all sizes, from domestic cats to endangered monkeys. For pet-related information, follow the link to Animal Advice where you'll find tips on common subjects including what to do if your school is giving away a goldfish as a prize or your neighbours' dog is barking. Also, if you're not sure if you want the responsibility of looking after a pet, you can adopt a virtual one to try before you buy. For slightly bigger animals, check out Born Free (www.bornfree.org.uk).

■ The rest of the best

Complete Hamster Site www.hamsters.co.uk

If you love hamsters, you can't help but love this shrine to the little wheel runners. There's a hamster e-zine, hamster facts, hamster pictures, hamster advice, hamster clubs and even a run-down of products for ... yes, you've guessed it, hamsters. For hamster fun without the straw and mess, check out Hamster Dance (www.nuttysites.com/rodent).

Pet Cat www.petcat.com

Feline lovers rejoice! Pet Cat contains everything you could possibly need to look after your cat. From virtual cat adoption and exclusive cat news to a yearly cat diary and e-kitty cards, it's a little obsessive but fun nonetheless.

Equiworld www.equiworld.net

If you love horses, you simply have to visit Equiworld, with its care and breeding information, horsy news, sporty stuff and loads more for both budding and existing riders. A definite winner for fans of the animals as well as the sports.

Equine World www.equine-world.co.uk

Not to be confused with Equiworld, this is a slightly less slick but no less interesting alternative to the big equestrian websites and is more than capable of holding its own with its well-written news, advice and articles which should delight any horse lover.

■ *The best of the rest*

Dogs Online www.dogsonline.co.uk

A wealth of fetching canine content and advice to prevent you from barking up the wrong tree (sorry).

Fish Keeping www.fishkeeping.co.uk

Keep your fish and one day they might keep you.

Pet Rabbits www.ukpet.rabbits.org.uk

Rabbits, rabbits, rabbits-rabbits-rabbits. Like a virtual Chaz and Dave song.

Online pet shops

Like a virtual Mr Macadoo of *Pigeon Street* fame, the internet is your complete one-stop pet shop. From fish food to dog collars, it's all here and you'll probably save a few quid into the bargain.

■ *The best of the best*

Pets Pyjamas **www.pets-pyjamas.co.uk**

Before you ask, we have no idea why it's called Pets Pyjamas. Silly name aside, this well-stocked pet supplies megasite offers a superb range of products as well as expert advice on care and feeding plus some captivating articles on a variety of different pet-related issues. Choosing your

products and placing an order couldn't be easier and delivery is suitably prompt, so you don't need to keep Spot or Snowy waiting.

■ *The rest of the best*

Pet Planet **www.petplanet.co.uk**

So much more than a pet shop, Pet Planet offer loads of information and advice on looking after pets as well as a virtual vet who will be happy to answer your animal health questions. When it comes to shopping, it's hard to complain – the site offers everything from catnip to dog insurance, and the Norwegian pine dog bed has to be seen to be believed. Pet Planet – pet paradise.

Petspark **www.petspark.co.uk**

Catering for cats and dogs, Petspark offers a decent range of toys, accessories and food to suit almost any breed and, more importantly, any budget. The design is pretty funky, too, with fun, games and a members' area to keep younger visitors happy, presumably so that they'll nag their parents to spend some money.

9

useful family advice

It's an unfortunate fact of life that things don't always go according to plan. You've probably heard the alarming statistic that one in three marriages ends in divorce – and plenty of those that don't will hit a rocky patch at some point. Even if your marriage is rock-steady, families can be hit with legal problems, money worries and bereavement and, while the internet can't offer a solution, there are plenty of sites to help you through those difficult times, or at least put you in touch with experts who can.

Marriage and relationship advice

'Till death do us part' is all well and good, but what if it all starts to go pear-shaped? Well, obviously there's no substitute for communication and trying to sort things out together but, if you need a little outside help, here's where to look.

■ *The best of the best*

Marriage Care **www.marriagecare.org.uk**
Marriage Care is a registered charity with one main purpose – to safeguard the institution of marriage and its

meaning in today's society. In order to help couples who might have run in to problems and advise those who haven't yet tied the knot, they have created an excellent resource packed full of help, support, reassurance and a wealth of advice on building and maintaining a strong family. There is a slight, albeit predictable, hint of moralising on the site – but if you are worried about the future of your relationship, this is an essential port of call.

■ The rest of the best

Relate www.relate.org.uk

Relate is probably the best-known organisation in the field of relationship counselling and, although its site is not as slick as Marriage Care, you'll find plenty of information on the organisation itself, what it can do for you and how to find your nearest counselling centre. Also, make sure you drop into the Relate bookshop for titles on marriage, sexual health, women's issues, bereavement and more.

Divorce.co.uk **www.divorce.co.uk**
If your marriage is beyond help and you decide that divorce is the only option, you'll probably want some advice on what to do and how to cope. Divorce.co.uk aims to help families 'manage their way through marriage breakdown, separation and divorce' and covers thorny issues such as deciding to end the relationship and telling your children, as well as offering practical advice and links to legal information.

Bereavement advice

If you're dealing with bereavement and grief, the last thing you'll probably think of doing is seeking help on the internet. Although the web can't provide a solution, there are plenty of sites which can put you in touch with someone who can, as well as offering advice on helping others cope with bereavement.

■ *The best of the best*

London Bereavement Network **www.bereavement.org.uk**
A no-frills guide to coping with grief and bereavement which, despite the name, is incredibly informative, no matter where you live. From practical advice on how to deal with the death of a loved one to academic discussion on the psychological effects of bereavement, the site covers almost

everything you could want (or need) to know. Also contains an excellent list of links to relevant sites and resources which is well worth a look.

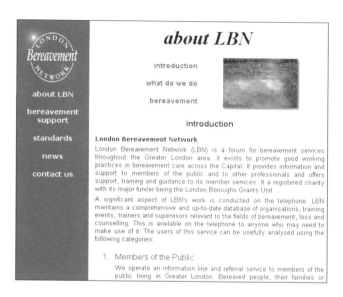

The rest of the best

The Centre for Grief Education **www.grief.org.au**

Australian site offering information about the centre itself as well as some extremely useful links to grief and bereavement sites on the internet.

Legal and financial advice

Most families will experience some sort of legal or money worries at some stage, so it's a good idea to be prepared for when they come along. Luckily, the web is full of information which will help you to cope with everything from minor legal squabbles to bankruptcy either by providing the advice you need free of charge online or by helping you to find a qualified solicitor or financial adviser to sort things out.

■ *The best of the best*

Law Rights **www.lawrights.co.uk**

If you don't mind paying a few quid for the privilege, you can get low-cost legal advice and documents to cover a wide range of legal issues on this excellent UK-focused site. Having said that, even if you'd rather not part with your hard-earned cash, there's still plenty of free information to give you an

idea of whether a case is worth fighting or if you haven't got a leg to stand on. Also if you want to take things further, there's a free lawyer referral service to get things moving. Simple but very very effective. For more of the same, check out Desktop Lawyer (**www.desktoplawyer.freeserve.net**).

■ *The rest of the best*

Find Law **www.findlaw.com**
Despite being based in the USA, Find Law is a great place to search for legal information, regardless of where you live. The site itself bears an uncanny resemblance to Yahoo! both in layout and structure, with a search box backed up by a browsable directory. Bear in mind that you will get plenty of American information, which is obviously very little use in English law, but it you dig deep enough, you'll almost certainly find what you need.

Trading Standards Net **www.tradingstandards.net**
If your legal problem is of a consumer nature – perhaps your washing machine has broken down for the billionth time, or your new shoes have dissolved in the rain – then you'll definitely want to check out Trading Standards Net. Not only does the site contain a wealth of advice on consumer rights, safety and quality standards, but there is also a message board to warn others of your experiences and information on where to turn for help. Bookmark this now – you never know when you'll need it.

This Is Money **www.thisismoney.com**
If your finances aren't quite as well oiled as you would like, then a visit to This Is Money should help you get back on

the right track. Offering advice on everything from shares to savings, pensions to personal loans, no matter what you need to know about money, it's almost certainly here. For a complete guide to money on the internet, pick up a copy of *The very best money websites*.

genealogy

You might know everything there is to know about your immediate family, but what about those long lost relatives and distant ancestors? No matter whether you are related to a famous historical character or that bloke who Francis Drake told to shove off until he'd finished his game of bowles – the internet makes it easier than ever to track them down.

Genealogy portals

If you're trying to track down your ancestors online, your first port of call should be one of the growing number of genealogy portals and directory sites. There are literally hundreds of thousands (possibly millions) of pages of genealogy information on the web, and it's the job of the portal to sort them neatly into an easy-to-browse format allowing you to get straight to the info you need. Some of them achieve this beautifully, some fail miserably – the ones listed here fall firmly into the first category.

■ The best of the best

Cyndi's List www.cyndislist.com

We must confess to being a little concerned about Cyndi. Not only is she clearly obsessed with genealogy, but she has also taken the time to collect and categorise over 73,000 online genealogy resources. Not that we're complaining, of course, as the site makes it easier than ever to find the information you need – using over 120 categories from unique peoples and cultures to ships' passenger lists and national dress. In short, if it's not here, you're not going to find it anywhere else.

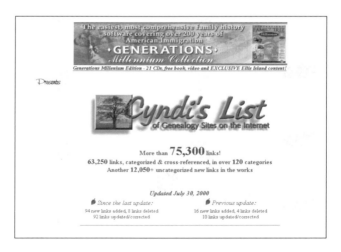

■ *The rest of the best*

Family Search www.familysearch.org

If Cyndi's List is all just a little too much for you, you might prefer the slick user-friendliness of Family Search from the Church of the Latter Day Saints. Using the service couldn't be easier: you simply type in as much information as possible about the person you're looking for and their immediate family and click the 'Search' button. If you get a match then it's a simple matter of choosing the records you need and downloading them to your computer. Job done.

Ancestry www.ancestry.com

The well-presented and utterly huge database of geneaology information makes it pretty straightforward to track down your Uncle Fred, no matter when or where he lived. The only minor drawbacks are the American bias of the information and also the fact that you have to pay for the results. It's great – if you don't mind parting with a few quid.

Family History www.familyhistory.com

Over 100,000 message boards, each focusing on a particular surname or set of surnames. Once you've tracked down your family board it's straightforward enough to start asking around for the information you need. It's worth noting that Family History has close ties with Ancestry, so don't be surprised if you click on a link and find yourself suddenly transported there.

UK-specific resources

The worldwide resources are all well and good, but it's all too easy to get swamped with American results which can throw you completely off the scent. There's no danger of that, however, if you stick to our recommended UK resources.

■ *The best of the best*

GENUKI www.genuki.org.uk

This wonderfully cluttered site is packed to the rafters with advice on tracking down UK and Irish ancestors online. Well-written guides to tracing relatives, information on genealogy in general and an extremely thorough set of links to relevant material and resources make this an essen-

tial port of call for experienced and first-time genealogists alike.

■ The rest of the best

The Society of Genealogists **www.sog.org.uk**

As the name of the site suggests, this is the official online home of a group of people who know one of two things about tracking down ancestors. Generously, they've decided to share some this knowledge with the rest of us in the form of well-written publications, information leaflets and, of course, this website. To be honest, there's not a great deal of information available on the site – but if you need a little help with your searching, these are definitely the people to speak to.

Scots Origins **www.origins.net**

No matter whether you're Scottish or just think you might have some ancestry north of the border, this is the place to start looking. Scots Origins is the official, governmental source of genealogical data for Scotland and, although there is a small charge (£6 at the time of writing) for using the service, the huge amount of information on offer makes it well worth the money. It looks pretty sharp, too.

■ The best of the rest

The Commonwealth War Graves Commission **www.cwgc.org**

Their name liveth evermore. Moving and informative in equal measures.

National Statistics **www.statistics.gov.uk**

The official source of information relating to hatches, matches and dispatches.

Still looking?

Although we've tried to cover the most useful and interesting online family resources, we're not infallible (hard to believe but true!).

If you can't find the information you're looking for then why not visit us on the web? The Zingin Family Guide (**www.zingin.com/guide/family**) contains all of the sites listed here plus an up-to-date directory of the best new resources for travellers and holidaymakers.

Don't panic if you're still having no luck, just come over to our Search Guide (**www.zingin.com/guide/search**) where our team of human search experts will try their hardest to help you out – and it won't cost you a penny!

quick reference guide

Dating

About Dating   dating.about.com   17
Dateline   www.dateline.uk.com   17
Dating Direct   www.datingdirect.com   18
Match   www.match.com   18
Lifestyle.UK Dating   www.lifestyle.co.uk/eh.htm   18
Personals 365   www.personals365.com   18
Secret Admirer   www.secretadmirer.com   16
Webpersonals   www.webpersonals.com   18

Marriage and weddings

Confetti   www.confetti.co.uk   19
Hitched   www.hitched.co.uk   20
Web Wedding   www.webwedding.co.uk   20
Wedding Circle   www.weddingcircle.com   21
Wedding Day   www.wedding-day.co.uk   20
Wedding Guide   www.weddingguide.co.uk   20

Pregnancy and childbirth

BPAS   www.bpas.org   24
Condomania   www.condomania.co.uk   24
FPA   www.fpa.org.uk   24

National Childbirth Trust   www.nct-online.org   24
Pregnancy Calendar   www.pregnancycalendar.com   23
The Baby Registry   www.thebabyregistry.co.uk   23

Child care

Baby World   www.babyworld.co.uk   27
E-Mum.com   www.e-mum.com   26
Missing Kids   www.missingkids.co.uk   27
My Family   www.myfamily.com   27
Parents Online   www.parents.org.uk   26
Urbia   www.urbia.co.uk   25
UK Parents   www.ukparents.co.uk   26

Health portals

BBC Health   www.bbc.co.uk/health   30
Dr Koop   www.drkoop.net   31
Health Gate UK   www.healthgate.co.uk   31
Health in Focus   www.healthinfocus.co.uk   30
Net Doctor   www.netdoctor.co.uk   29
NHS Direct   www.nhsdirect.nhs.uk   30
Surgery Door   www.surgerydoor.co.uk   30

Specific health advice

Achoo   www.achoo.com   34
Alcoholics Anonymous   www.alcoholics-anonymous.org.uk   33
British Heart Foundation   www.bhf.org.uk   32
Diabetic Association   www.diabetes.org.uk   33
First Aid   members.tripod.co.uk/rescue   31
Imperial Cancer Research Fund   www.icnet.uk   34

Internet Mental Health   www.mentalhealth.com 34
Meningitis Research Foundation   www.meningitis.org.uk 32
Pfizer   www.pfizer.com 34
RNIB   www.rnib.org.uk 33
Samaritans   www.samaritans.org 33

Healthy eating

British Nutrition Foundation   www.nutrition.org.uk 34
The Food Foundation   www.fooddirectory.co.uk 35
My Nutrition   www.mynutrition.co.uk 35
Weight Watchers   uk.weightwatchers.com 36

Health and beauty shopping

All Cures   www.allcures.com 36
Avon   www.uk.avon.com 38
Boots   www.boots.co.uk 37
Iris Online   www.iris-online.co.uk 38
Look Fantastic   www.lookfantastic.com 38
Condomania   www.condomania.co.uk 38

Education portals

Advisory Centre For Education   www.ace-ed.org.uk 43
BBC Education   www.bbc.co.uk/education 40
Education Unlimited   www.educationunlimited.co.uk 42
Eduweb   www.eduweb.co.uk 44
European schoolnet   www.eun.org 42
Learnfree   www.learnfree.co.uk 41
Parentline Plus   www.parentlineplus.org.uk 43
Schools Net   www.schoolsnet.com 42

Search Gate   www.searchgate.co.uk 42
Times Educational Supplement   www.tes.co.uk 43
Top Marks   www.topmarks.co.uk 42
The National Grid for Learning   www.ngfl.gov.uk 43

Pre-school and infants

Big Brainy Babies   www.brainybabies.com 46
Coloring   www.coloring.com 46
Fun School   www.funschool.com 44
Mamamedia   www.mamamedia.com 45
Tellytubbies   www.bbc.co.uk/education/teletubbies 45
Tweenies   www.bbc.co.uk/education/tweenies 46
Winnie the Pooh   www.winniethepooh.co.uk 46

Primary school

Ask Jeeves for Kids   www.ajkids.com 48
Bonus   www.bonus.com 48
Homework Solver   www.homeworksolver.com 49
Parents Online   www.parents.org.uk 47
Surf Monkey   www.surfmonkey.com 49
Web 66   web66.coled.umn.edu 50
Yahooligans!   www.yahooligans.com 49
Yucky   www.yucky.com 49

Secondary school

A Levels   www.a-levels.co.uk 52
BBC Bitesize GCSE   www.bbc.co.uk/education/revision 51
Discovery Channel   www.discovery.com 53
History Channel   www.historychannel.com 53

Maths Help   www.maths-help.co.uk 53
New Scientist   www.newscientist.com 53
Project GCSE   www.projectgcse.co.uk 52
Revise It   www.reviseit.com 52
The Learning Shop   www.learningshop.com 53

Further and higher education

Edunet   www.edunet.com 56
Hobsons   www.hobsons.co.uk 55
Info Youth   www.infoyouth.com 56
Student Loans Company   www.slc.co.uk 56
The National Union of Students   www.nus.org.uk 55
UCAS   www.ucas.ac.uk 54
Unofficial Guides   www.unofficial-guides.com 56

General reference tools

Ask A Librarian   www.earl.org.uk/ask 60
Britannica   www.britannica.com 57
Dictionary   www.dictionary.com 59
Encarta   www.encarta.com 58
Encyclopedia.com   www.encyclopedia.com 60
Funk and Wagnall's   www.funkandwagnalls.com 61
Google   www.google.com 61
Multimap   www.multimap.com 60
The Virtual Reference Desk   www.refdesk.com 59
Travlang   www.travlang.com 59
Thesaurus   www.thesaurus.com 59
xrefer   www.xrefer.com 58

Job hunting

Big Blue Dog   www.bigbluedog.com 64
Gisajob   www.gisajob.com 63
Job Search   www.jobsearch.co.uk 65
Jobs Unlimited   www.jobsunlimited.co.uk 65
Monster   www.monster.co.uk 62
Reed   www.reed.co.uk 65
Revolver   www.revolver.com 65
Stepstone   www.stepstone.co.uk 64
Top Jobs   www.topjobs.co.uk 64

Useful employment-related resources

CV Special   www.cvspecial.co.uk 66
I-Resign.com   www.i-resign.com 65
One CV   www.one-cv.com 67

Sites for men

Boots for Men   www.boots-men.co.uk 71
Boys Stuff   www.boysstuff.co.uk 71
Firebox   www.firebox.com 71
Guy Rules   www.guyrules.com 71
FHM   www.fhm.com 70
GQ   www.swoon.com/mag_rack/gq.html 70
Maxim   www.maxim-magazine.co.uk 71
mens-care.org   www.mens-care.org 69
Men's Health   www.menshealth.co.uk 70
The English Shaving Company www.theenglishshavingcompany.co.uk 71
Uploaded   www.uploaded.com 70

Sites for women

Accessorize	www.accessorize.co.uk	74
BEME	www.beme.com	74
Charlotte Street	www.charlottestreet.co.uk	74
Gal Rules	www.galrules.com	75
Handbag	www.handbag.com	72
iCircle	www.icircle.co.uk	73
PS Magazine	www.psmagazine.co.uk	74
Vogue	www.vogue.co.uk	75
Women.com	www.women.com	73

Sites for kids

Aardman Animations	www.aardman.com	78
Action Man	www.actionman.com	78
Barbie	www.barbie.com	78
Children's BBC	www.bbc.co.uk/cbbc	75
CIA Homepage for Kids	www.odci.gov/cia/ciakids	79
CITV	www.citv.co.uk	76
Disney	disney.go.com	77
KidsCom	www.kidscom.com	77
Kids Channel	www.kids-channel.co.uk	77
KidsJokes	www.kidsjokes.com	78
Kids' Space	www.kids-space.org	77
Kids Travel	www.kidstravel.co.uk	78
National Geographic Kids	www.nationalgeographic.com/kids	78
Pixar	www.pixar.com	78
Pokémon World	www.pokemon.com	78
Sesame Street	www.sesamestreet.com	78
The Simpsons	www.thesimpsons.com	77

Thunk www.thunk.com 78
Warner Brothers www.kids.warnerbros.com 77

Sites for teenagers

Irn Bru www.irn-bru.co.uk 81
Monster Teenzone teenzone.monster.co.uk 81
Nothing Pink www.nothingpink.com 80
Phat Start www.phatstart.com 80
Riot Grrl www.riotgrrl.com 80
Teen Chat www.teenchat.co.uk 81
Teen Today www.teentoday.co.uk 80
The Site www.thesite.org.uk 79

Sites for students

Funny www.funny.co.uk 84
Hot Toast www.hot-toast.co.uk 83
Napster www.napster.com 84
Red Mole www.redmole.co.uk 83
Rough Guides travel.roughguides.com 84
Student Net www.student-net.co.uk 82
Student UK www.studentuk.com 83
Student World www.student-world.co.uk 83
TV Cream www.tv.cream.org 84
The Ultimate Band List www.ubl.com 85

Sites for seniors

Active Lives www.activelives.co.uk 86
Hairnet www.hairnet.org 87
My Hairnet www.myhairnet.com 87

Saga   www.saga.co.uk 86
Silver Surfers   www.silversurfers.net 87
Vavo.com   www.vavo.com 85
Women Over 50   www.wo50.com 87

Sites for gays and lesbians

About Gay Life   gaylife.about.com 88
Gay.com (UK)   uk.gay.com 89
Gay Life UK   www.gaylifeuk.com 89
Gay Times   www.gaytimes.co.uk 90
Lesbian Nation   www.lesbianation.com 89
Planet Out   www.planetout.com 89
Queer Resources Directory   www.qrd.org 90

Animal advice

Born Free   www.bornfree.org.uk 92
Complete Hamster Site   www.hamsters.co.uk 92
Dogs Online   www.dogsonline.co.uk 93
Equine World   www.equine-world.co.uk 93
Equiworld   www.equiworld.net 93
Fish Keeping   www.fishkeeping.co.uk 93
Hamster Dance   www.nuttysites.com/rodent 92
Pet Cat   www.petcat.com 93
Pet Rabbits   www.ukpet.rabbits.org.uk 93
RSPCA   www.rspca.org.uk 91

Online pet shops

Pet Planet   www.petplanet.co.uk 95
Petspark   www.petspark.co.uk 95
Pets Pyjamas   www.pets-pyjamas.co.uk 94

Marriage and relationship advice

Divorce.co.uk   **www.divorce.co.uk** 98
Marriage Care   **www.marriagecare.org.uk** 96
Relate   **www.relate.org.uk** 97

Bereavement advice

London Bereavement Network   **www.bereavement.org.uk** 98
The Centre for Grief Education **www.grief.org.au** 99

Legal and financial advice

Desktop Lawyer   **www.desktoplawyer.freeserve.net** 101
Find Law   **www.findlaw.com** 101
Law Rights   **www.lawrights.co.uk** 100
This Is Money   **www.thisismoney.com** 101
Trading Standards Net **www.tradingstandards.net** 101

Genealogy portals

Ancestry   **www.ancestry.com** 105
Cyndi's List   **www.cyndislist.com** 104
Family History   **www.familyhistory.com** 105
Family Search   **www.familysearch.org** 105

UK-specific genealogy resources

CWGC   **www.cwgc.org** 107
GENUKI   **www.genuki.org.uk** 106
Scots Origins   **www.origins.net** 107

The Society of Genealogists   **www.sog.org.uk**   107
National Statistics   **www.statistics.gov.uk**   108

Zingin links

Feedback (Email)   **feedback@zingin.com**
Feedback (Form)   **www.zingin.com/feedback.html**
Home   **www.zingin.com**   vi
Search Guide   **www.zingin.com/guide/search**   108
Suggest a Site   **www.zingin.com/add.html**
Family Guide   **www.zingin.com/guide/family**   108